D0468243

ALSO BY TOM LACALAMITA

The Ultimate Bread Machine Cookbook

The Ultimate Pasta Machine Cookbook

TOM LACALAMITA

PHOTOGRAPHS BY SIMON METZ

ILLUSTRATIONS BY LAURIE DAVIS

SIMON & SCHUSTER

New York • London • Toronto • Sydney • Tokyo • Singapore

The Ultimate Espresso Machine Cookbook

SIMON & SCHUSTER
Rockefeller Center
1230 Avenue of the Americas
New York, NY 10020

Designed by Eve Metz/Elina Nudelman

Manufactured in the United States of America

1 3 5 7 9 10 8 6 4 2

Library of Congress Cataloging-in-Publication Data
Lacalamita, Tom.
The ultimate espresso machine cookbook / Tom Lacalamita.
p. cm.
Includes index.
1. Cookery (Coffee). 2. Espresso. I. Title.
TX819.C6L33 1995
641.6'373—dc20 95-42724
CIP
ISBN 0-684-81336-X

For Yayi and Cristina

ACKNOWLEDGMENTS

To Bill Rosen, for the opportunity to do this book. To my editor, Gillian Casey Sowell, for her guidance and support. And to the rest of the Simon & Schuster team—Frank Metz, Jackie Seow, Eve Metz, and Toni Rachiele—for their respective contributions along the path of this book's creation.

To Simon Metz and A.J. Battifarano, for their beautiful portrayal of the drinks and desserts on film. And Laurie Davis, for the skillful illustrations.

Sincere thanks to my special friend Glenna Vance, for the nutritional analyses, enthusiasm, and support.

Special thanks to Elizabeth Kane and Mitchel Margulis of Lavazza Premium Coffees for providing me with expert information on espresso and coffee and for always finding the time to answer my endless questions.

My sincere appreciation to all of the manufacturers and companies credited on page 154 for providing the equipment and technical information needed in developing this book. A special thanks to Julia Stambules for always sending me whatever I needed, when it was needed.

And most important, to my family and friends, for sharing with me my love of food and for the knowledge and skills they have so graciously provided me over the years.

CONTENTS

FOREWORD

Until just recently, Americans had almost no choice in the coffee that they were drinking. They could pick from what was available in the local supermarket or order up the murky brown urn-coffee that was dished out in six-ounce portions at local take-out establishments, but that was about it. Now, all that has changed. Finally, Americans have begun to rediscover coffee as it has been enjoyed around the world for centuries—not just as a jolt of caffeine to help us through the day but as a rich, complex beverage worthy of serious culinary consideration.

The emergence of a coffee culture in North America found its origins in the Pacific Northwest city of Seattle. What started out there with a few small mom-and-pop operations has blossomed into numerous coffee retailers, nationwide chains of espresso bars, and sophisticated, independent establishments that provide excellent coffee and a congenial atmosphere.

As we have learned to appreciate good coffee, we have also seen an increased interest in preparing and serving the same high-quality coffee and coffee drinks at home. No other coffee has been more affected by this than espresso. Originally of Italian origin, espresso coffee and machines for home use in this country have been increasing steadily in sales over the past few years. In fact, it is estimated that at least 8.3 million American households already own an espresso machine and that 43 percent of them use the appliance frequently.

Because of advances in technology and design, the home espresso machines available today are far superior to anything we have seen in the past. The home *barista* (the Italian name given to the professional who brews espresso in a café) is now capable of brewing espresso with a fine head of crema, the thick, golden foam that is the sign of a well-made cup of espresso, and of frothing milk to make a thick, airy head.

After having worked with various cooking appliances and their manufacturers for the past ten years, I decided to try my hand to see if even I could make the quintessential cup of espresso. The happy results then inspired me to experiment further. With the assistance of numerous companies and individuals, I was able to put together an impressive collection of espresso machines. By combining my professional experience, my knowledge of small electric appliances, and my background as a cookbook author and food writer, I at once put these machines to the test and began compiling this selection of traditional and contemporary drink and dessert recipes.

This collection of recipes has been triple-tested using sixteen of the most popular espresso machines. I have also provided step-by-step instructions on how to achieve the best results from your espresso machine, along with practical troubleshooting information.

When using this book, be sure to measure carefully, use the very best espresso coffee and ingredients available, and above all, get to know your espresso machine by reading all the materials provided by your manufacturer. Once you get the hang of it, you may wonder how you ever lived without your daily espresso or latte.

INTRODUCTION

THE HISTORY OF COFFEE

No other beverage has aroused as much suspicion and led to as much treachery as coffee. Although taken for granted by most of us as our daily morning beverage or midday pick-me-up, coffee has been documented throughout history as the cause of rebellions, assassinations, endless espionage plots, schemes, and acts of treason. What began simply as the fruit of a tree growing wild on the plains of Africa and in the remote valleys of Arabia has evolved over the centuries into a highly valued commodity that is traded on the world markets alongside petroleum, steel, and grain; indeed, the economies and wealth of entire nations are based solely on the unpretentious coffee bean.

No one knows for certain when coffee was first discovered and used. From early writings, however, we do know that it was originally thought to have mysterious curing powers. As far back as A.D. 1000, the renowned Arabic physician Abu ibn Sina, or Avicenna as he is known in Western history, learned of the stimulating properties of the then extremely rare coffee bean. Avicenna administered medicinal tonics to important Arab dignitaries, brewed from coffee beans traded by the caravans from Arabic outposts in Upper Egypt and Libya. Nevertheless, it is believed that coffee, a plant native to what is today Ethiopia, was first cultivated and used in Africa not as a beverage but as a food, with early tribes mixing the ripe cherries from the coffee tree with animal fat for use as a source of protein and nourishment. Not until later was it brewed with cold water into a form of wine.

The coffee tree is believed to have been brought to the Middle East from the ancient country of Kaffa in Abyssinia by the Queen of Sheba and her subjects on their way to Israel to meet the Jewish king, Solomon. Some of the Queen's descendants eventually settled for a period of time in what is today Yemen, therefore establishing an explanation for how this African plant found its way to the Middle East, where it was to gain great favor.

The origins of the cup of coffee as we know it today may date back to the fifteenth century. According to a popular story, around 1400 a young Yemeni goatherd who was employed at a monastery of devout Muslims observed his goats reacting strangely after eating the reddish fruit of low-growing bushes in a remote spot where they were grazing. Rather than resting tranquilly at night, the goats were restless and frisky. The goatherd reported his findings to the imam, but when the monk tried eating the ripe fruit he found it unpalatable. Knowing that certain grains improve in flavor when cooked, he tried roasting the pit of the coffee cherry, which he then crushed and mixed with water to form a paste. Since the rich-tasting mixture was bitter, the monk added some honey to soften the flavor, and the food's effect on him was like nothing he had ever felt before. The mixture gave him a greater level of awareness and warded off drowsiness once night had fallen. When the midnight hour of prayer arrived, he was the only member of the community capable of remaining fully awake. Believing the potion he had taken to be miraculous, he shared it with the other monks, who were so impressed that they called this wonderful brew *kawah,* which in Arabic means "that which excites and causes the spirits to rise." Coffee acquired an almost mystical role and was soon used by participants in all-night religious ceremonies throughout the Muslim world. In order to keep up with the growing demand, cultivation of coffee was established and developed into a highly lucrative industry.

The similarities in sound among the word *coffee* in English, *caffè* in Italian, *café* in Spanish or French, and *Kaffee* in German has led linguists to believe that the name derives from either the ancient Abyssinian country *Kaffa* or from the Arabic word *kawah.* Regardless of its etymological origins, once coffee began to lose its religious associations and word of its stimulating effects spread among scholars, the beverage rapidly became popular throughout the Islamic world.

Over the course of time, the Arabs refined the process for brewing coffee, improving upon its flavor. This process involved removing and discarding the fruit that encapsulated the seeds, or "beans," roasting the beans, and then grinding them to a fine powder, which was steeped in water. The resulting mixture was then reduced over heat by 50 percent. Since wine and other alcoholic beverages were prohibited in the Islamic world, *gahveh khaneh,* or coffeehouses, became the center of social life during the sixteenth century. Nevertheless, they were looked upon by many with suspicion. Since people no longer had to go to religious centers to consume coffee, the clerics were alarmed by the consequent decline in attendance at religious services. Government officials were also distressed that many people were gathering in coffeehouses, where they discussed the events of the day, a situation viewed as subversive. As a result, various Arabic governments attempted, on many occasions, to shut down the coffeehouses. Apparently, the Sultan Amurat III, who facilitated his accession to power by murdering his five brothers, was the first to close down the coffeehouses of Constantinople, torturing their proprietors to avoid any subversive sentiments or discussions. Popular demand, however, was so strong that eventually the coffeehouses reopened, only to be closed once again, even more brutally. Mahomet Kolpili, an official of the Ottoman Empire, was so distressed to see people sneaking back to the closed coffeehouses that he had them destroyed and the proprietors, along with their determined customers, thrown to their death in the Bosporus. The demand for coffee on the part of Ottoman society was so unmitigated, however—and the revenue from heavy taxes on coffee so great—that eventually public sentiment won out and coffeehouses were permitted to reopen. The beverage's influence began to spread even wider around this time as coffee now began to be brewed and served in private homes. In fact, it played such an important role in everyday life that Ottoman wives could divorce their husbands if they were unable to provide them with the beloved beverage.

During this time of the Ottoman Empire's expansionist activities throughout Arabia and Europe, the cultivation, trade, and widespread diffusion of coffee was closely controlled by the empire. As a result, besides being subjected to Ottoman rule, the conquered peoples under their control were also to fall under the spell of the wondrous, intoxicating beverage called coffee.

COFFEE IN EUROPE

Coffee was first introduced into Europe by Venetian traders, who picked it up when calling on Ottoman ports. Christianity, however, did not embrace the arrival of this Islamic beverage with open arms. In fact, the sixteenth-century Catholic church looked upon coffee as the drink of the devil and suggested that Catholics risked eternal damnation if they were to drink it. After much controversy, however, Pope Clement VIII decided to taste the beverage for himself before making any final determinations. Rumor has it that the pope was so taken by the heady aroma and flavor that he declared that anything so good could not possibly be the work of the devil and that to prohibit its partaking would be a sin. And so, small, plainly attired coffeehouses were soon opening in the port cities of the Italian city-states.

While coffee had spread rapidly throughout the Arabic world by means of the coffeehouses, in Europe its consumption first spread mainly by way of street vendors, who added it to their offerings of cold fruit beverages, dried fruits, and nuts. Peddlers who regularly carried basic household goods and foodstuffs also prepared and sold brewed coffee from house to house. Unfortunately for the Europeans, the export of coffee and its prices were strictly controlled by the Eastern ports in an effort to monopolize its distribution. But as the Ottoman Empire began to crumble during the sixteenth century, opportunists seized upon the occasion to make their fortune from the coffee left behind by the retreating Ottomans. The most famous of these enterprising entrepreneurs was a Pole, Franz George Kolschitzky, whose opportunity arrived in 1683, when the Polish king, Jan Sobieski, defeated the Turks during the siege of Vienna. As the Ottoman forces retreated, they left behind many riches, including hundreds of pounds of green coffee beans, or "Turkish corn," as it was referred to by the victors. Kolschitzky, who had once been a Turkish captive, recognized that the "Turkish corn" was none other than raw coffee, worth a small fortune, and he graciously offered to take it off the hands of the victorious soldiers, who readily accepted. With this quick-witted move, Kolschitzky was rapidly on his way to establishing himself as the king of coffee in Vienna, and he soon opened the first Viennese coffeehouse, the Blue Bottle. Within a few years, the industrious Kolschitzky was the proud proprietor of several coffeehouses throughout Central Europe, with the beverage, now adapted to European tastes, being prepared and served with whipped cream and made into ices.

Not too far away, in France, Francesco Procopio dei Coltelli, a fallen Sicilian nobleman turned ambulant coffee peddler, heard of Kolschitzky's good fortune and decided to try his hand at opening up Paris's first coffeehouse. Procopio's affluent *salon de caffè* was well received by Parisians, who could now enjoy coffee in a luxurious environment along with a menu of other foods and beverages. The concept of the European coffeehouse rapidly spread throughout Europe along with the beverage's popularity, and as it did, so, too, did the desire to end the Arabic monopoly on its distribution.

COFFEE IN THE AMERICAS

Little by little, European and Muslim traders and spies succeeded in smuggling coffee seedlings and cuttings out of Arabia and tried their hands at growing the precious plants in other tropical environments. The Dutch established their first coffee plantations in their Indonesian colonies of Batavia and Java, efforts that proved to be extremely successful. The Dutch also shared coffee seedlings that they had grown in the Botanical Gardens of Leyden with the royalty of Europe. In fact, as an act of conciliation, the Dutch presented Louis XVI of France with a coffee plant at the signing of the peace accord in Utrecht, not knowing that this single act of friendship would hold the key to the future of the coffee industry in America.

The events that led to the introduction of coffee into the New World began when a French naval officer stationed in the French colony of Martinique, Captain Gabriel des Clieux, learned of the success of the Dutch coffee plantations and dreamed of establishing the same on Martinique. After purported intrigues, thievery, and a tête-à-tête with the wife of a high-ranking government official, des Clieux came to possess a cutting from the royal Jardin des Plantes, only to encounter numerous obstacles in getting his prized possession to the Caribbean. On board the ship, a Dutch spy tried to protect Holland's control of coffee distribution by attempting to destroy the cutting. Later in the journey, attacks on the vessel by the Royal Spanish Navy almost brought des Clieux's plan to an end.

But the most dangerous blow of all was the loss of most of the potable water on the vessel after a fierce ocean storm. The situation became so desperate that the passengers were rationed only a few drops of water a day. Rather than let his cutting dry up, des Clieux shared his ration with his botanical charge. Fortunately for des Clieux, his efforts were well rewarded—the cutting flourished in the tropical climate of Martinique, and the French were now able to establish their first coffee plantations in the New World, plantations that would later spread to their other colonies.

But the story does not end here. Not unlike the Dutch and the Arabs, the French jealously protected their stake in the developing coffee industry and outlawed the export of plants or cuttings under penalty of death. The other great colonizers and traders of the world, particularly the Portuguese and the Spanish, were also interested in starting their own coffee plantations in their American colonies but lacked the much-needed plants. But a diplomatic favor and a romantic liaison in 1772 opened the door for the Portuguese. That year, the French and Dutch governments asked the Portuguese viceroy of Brazil to send a neutral emissary to assist them in settling a territorial dispute in Guiana. After assisting the two rival nations in resolving their differences, the Portuguese envoy, Francisco de Melo Palheta, succeeded in seducing the French viceroy's wife. On the day of his departure for Brazil, the viceroy's wife presented him with a token of her affection: a bouquet of native flowers, hidden in the midst of which he found fresh coffee tree cuttings. Brazil now had the makings for what would turn it into the world's largest and most important producer of coffee.

Over the next two centuries coffee became the one cash crop that could either make or break governments and national economies. During periods of good harvests, coffee-growing nations prospered. Overplanting and blights, however, were capable of destroying entire plantations, industries, and economies, as happened in Asia during the nineteenth century. The Dutch coffee growers and traders in Indonesia controlled for the most part the entire coffee industry worldwide. Unfortunately for them, in 1878, a quick-traveling disease struck their coffee plantations and in a few short years the entire industry, which had been developed over two centuries, was wiped out completely. Brazil escaped the blight and was suddenly in place to become the leading producer of coffee, a position that, although not without its troubles, it still maintains today, accounting for over 25 percent of the world's coffee production. Brazil had all of the appropriate primary resources for growing coffee: vast stretches of fertile land, a tropical climate, and a cheap labor supply—slaves supplemented by immigrants from Europe. Coffee growing flourished in Brazil, but not without taking its toll. In the late 1800s, Emperor Pedro II of Brazil freed the country's slaves, who had provided most of the manpower for tending the coffee plantations—an act that doomed him to be the last monarch of his country. Because of this change, which radically affected the Brazilian coffee industry, the emperor was forced to abdicate and Brazil became a democracy. Nevertheless, by the early 1900s Brazil was soon bordering on bankruptcy due to overplanting, a migration of workers to the cities, and most of all a worldwide coffee glut. A need for government control over the growing and distribution of coffee was apparent. After various economic disasters, including the worldwide economic depression of the 1930s, the country was forced to cut back on production by destroying 25 million bags of coffee beans (well over 3 billion pounds) and 1.5 billion coffee trees.

Between 1940 and 1972 various accords to apply production and price controls were agreed upon by the major coffee-producing countries of Central and South America and the United States, which after World War II had become the center of worldwide coffee distribution. Coffee production and prices began to stabilize, but in 1972 prices began to fluctuate and all controls disappeared. Coffee soon became a speculative commodity, traded on the world markets like petroleum and steel.

While no coffee is grown in the continental United States (a small amount of Kona coffee is produced in Hawaii), coffee has been a part of our culture since the early 1600s, when the first Dutch and English colonists arrived. In fact, a coffee grinder was part of the cargo list of the *Mayflower*. Coffee, as well as other imported items, was heavily taxed by the British, although the dumping of tea into Boston Harbor by the fledgling American revolutionaries aided the spread of affordable coffee in the colonies. The Dutch and French, archenemies of the English, could not have been more pleased with the chance to provide the colonists with an inexpensive and steady supply of coffee. Eventually, coffee became even more popular than ale, which had been the breakfast beverage of choice. Other factors that contributed to converting America into a country of coffee drinkers include free trade with European colonies after independence from Britain and the influx of coffee-drinking European immigrants during the 1800s and early 1900s.

Up until the early 1960s the United States remained a major consumer of coffee. Numbers started to drop dramatically, however, during the soft drink revolution, and another swift blow to American coffee consumption came with the devastation of the Brazilian coffee crop in 1975 by a killer frost: over the next two years wholesale prices of the choice arabica coffee beans rose over 500 percent. In order to maintain prices, coffee companies were forced to use a higher concentration of what are known as robusta coffee beans from Africa, causing a sharp decline in the quality and taste of the coffee. Almost an entire generation of Americans grew up thinking that coffee should have an offensive, bitter taste and that it was something that you made with a kettle of boiling water and a jar of freeze-dried brown powder. On a more positive note, the mass production and consumption of low-quality coffee created a niche for an entire specialty coffee industry that was to develop and grow to unbelievable proportions. Small purveyors of coffee were able to capitalize on this burgeoning market, which over the past twenty years has turned into a multibillion-dollar-a-year industry and has elevated coffee to the popular status it enjoys today.

GROWING COFFEE

The unpretentious but prized coffee plant, which in 1990 constituted approximately a $12 billion-a-year industry worldwide for beans alone, is a member of the Rubiaceae family and is a close cousin of the jasmine and gardenia plants. This is not surprising if you have ever smelled the fragrant flower of this tropical plant. Of the approximately sixty different species of coffee, two are most important: *Coffea arabica*, which is grown in twenty-five different countries and accounts for 70 percent of the world's coffee production, and *Coffea cannephora*, or, as it is most commonly known, robusta, which makes up the balance of production and is grown primarily in twelve African countries.

Coffee trees grow best in hot, wet, temperate environments. They seem to thrive in rocky, hilly conditions at altitudes ranging from 2,000 to 3,900 feet. It takes approximately four to five years for a coffee plant to mature into a fruit-bearing tree that will flower and produce either once or twice a year, depending on growing conditions. The reddish-brown clustered fruits of the tree—the cherries, as they are called—each contain two seeds coupled together, which form the beans. Stripping the cherries of the fleshy fruit, the beans are revealed under a parchment-like covering. Removing this reveals the bluish-green, raw arabica coffee beans or orange-green robusta beans. On average, *Coffea arabica* trees bear just under a pound to over four pounds of beans, while approximately one pound of beans can be harvested from the *Coffea cannephora* (robusta). Depending upon the topical conditions where the trees grow, the cherries are either hand picked or stripped from the trees by machinery. Since the fruit matures at different times, the time- and labor-intensive hand-picking method is preferred, for the picker chooses only those cherries that are ripe, whereas stripping removes both ripened and green cherries at the same time.

As a fruit, the ripe coffee cherries contain natural sugars. If the picked coffee is allowed to sit around for more than a couple of days, it will begin to ferment, which can adversely affect the flavor of the beans. The beans, therefore, must be removed as soon as possible, according to one of two methods. The most labor-intensive and expensive technique is called the *wet process,* which is usually how hand-picked beans are processed. Within two days of being picked, the ripe fruit is removed from the cherry by hand and the green beans are then allowed to ferment two to four days, after which they are washed, dried, and sorted. Raw coffee beans processed by this method produce a more expensive, mellowed cup of coffee and are referred to as *washed coffees.* Most of the coffee produced in the remote, mountainous regions of Colombia, where machinery cannot be used, are processed this way. The more common *dry process* is typically used with stripped coffee and most commonly characterizes the way coffees from Brazil and West Africa are processed. Following this system, the ripe and green cherries are washed and then spread out to dry in direct sunlight for approximately fifteen to twenty days. Afterward, the beans are separated from the dried fruit and allowed to dry before sorting. At this point, the processed green coffee beans, eventually sold as *natural coffees,* are placed in sacks for shipment to specific customers or for sale on the coffee commodities markets of New York or London.

PREPARING COFFEE FOR MARKET

The coffee we ultimately buy is either a blend of different types of varietals, such as arabica and robusta, or are a single varietal, like the popular 100 percent arabica. Even with the latter, however, the beans are mixed and blended according to their characteristics, which are determined by origin and the method by which they were processed. For example, *washed arabica* has acidic, aromatic qualities, while *natural arabica* is sweeter and more full-bodied. Coffee companies have specific standards and flavors that they strive to achieve when they are producing their coffee.

As the imam and the goatherd discovered back in Yemen, the chemical composition of green coffee beans changes when roasted, radically altering the flavor. Heat applied to green beans is conducted by the bean's natural water content, passing from cell to cell. But rather than shrink in size, the beans expand, causing them to shed their natural outer skin. As the beans heat, they also begin to change color from their natural hue to a yellowish brown and finally to a rich, dark brown. During this process, the chemical composition of the coffee bean is also changing, causing the natural sugars and proteins to interact with each other in a fashion that brings out the unique, distinct flavor of the coffee.

During the roasting process, the beans increase in size anywhere from 25 to 50 percent, while losing 15 to 20 percent of their weight. The caffeine content of the beans is not affected significantly by roasting. In fact, the amount of caffeine is determined by the species of coffee (arabica or robusta), as well as its variety and origin. Robusta, for example, generally has two to three times more caffeine than arabica. The depth of color and flavor of the coffee beans, on the other hand, is determined by the length of the roasting process, which also affects the acidity and body of the coffee. During roasting, the heat releases and intensifies the natural oils that give coffee its rich distinctive aroma and flavor. The ultimate character desired in the coffee determines the length of the roasting process. Since, for example, espresso drinkers want a richer, more full-bodied cup of coffee, beans for espresso are roasted longer. After the coffee beans have been sufficiently roasted, they are then rapidly air cooled to halt the roasting process. Be aware, however, that very dark coffee beans are usually a sign of overroasting, as are beans that are very oily. Coffee brewed from those beans will have a burnt, bitter taste since the coffee has passed its maximum flavor potential and the beans are most likely also to be rancid.

There are two basic roasting methods. The older, more traditional method involves drum roasting the green beans over an external heat source. The beans are turned over and over again, roasting as they make direct contact with the hot metal of the drum. The newer, more exact method is to roast the beans with hot air in cylindrical metal tumblers. As the chamber spins, centrifugal force lifts the beans into suspension and they roast in the hot convection air. The advantage of this process is that the beans never come in direct contact with the hot metal of the roasting chamber and are, therefore, roasted more evenly.

The best characteristics of coffee, like those of good wines, are achieved from blending. In order to obtain a certain flavor, the master coffee blender tests different lots and types of beans to determine the fullness of their taste, as well as their body, acidity, and sweetness. Arabica coffee, for instance, is smoother and less robust than robusta, which is too strong for most tastes to be sold straight (although it can be found in most coffees marketed for the Hispanic market). For a more full-bodied espresso blend, then, usually good-quality arabica is blended with a certain percentage of robusta. This is not to say that 100 percent arabica coffee, which by the way is the most popular blend of espresso and drip coffee sold in the United States, will not do well in an espresso machine. Remember, the blender can and will mix different types of arabica from different parts of the world to achieve the right combination.

Coffee blends include beans of different sizes, shapes, and color; arabica beans, for example, are more elongated than the rounder robusta. And different beans are roasted for different periods of time to achieve a certain flavor and aroma. Buying quality coffee from a reputable specialty coffee retailer or buying a well-known, high-quality brand should at least give you a 50 percent chance of brewing success. The other 50 percent depends upon proper grinding, preparation, and storage of any leftover coffee.

As you begin to explore the world of coffee, you will see that there are many different varieties, blends, and brands available for use in espresso machines. The best way to determine the one you enjoy most is to experiment. When trying a new coffee, always purchase the smallest quantity possible. Write down what you enjoyed or disliked about it, and keep on exploring until you come across your favorite.

THE HISTORY OF ESPRESSO

When the Arabs first began to brew coffee, they did so in bell-shaped copper pots called *ibriks*. The finely ground coffee was boiled three times with water, sugar, and any spices the maker desired to add. The prepared beverage was poured, grounds and all, into small cups, and after the grounds had settled to the bottom of the cups, the thick brew was ready to drink. This method, which continues to be used in parts of the old Ottoman Empire and in northern Europe, was also adhered to in Europe and the Americas for hundreds of years, even though coffee drinkers suspected that there had to be an easier, more convenient way to enjoy their favorite beverage. Eventually the French began to filter the coffee before pouring it, but the basic brewing method of boiling did not change. Not until the invention of the percolator did coffee preparation change radically. The only problem was that percolated coffee didn't—and still doesn't—really taste very good and was not as thick as the type of coffee previously enjoyed by the Europeans. Furthermore, by cycling the boiling water over and over the grounds, percolated coffee was bitter and would at times even taste cooked if not burnt.

In the 1840s, a Scottish inventor named Robert Napier developed a method of vacuum-brewing coffee. In principle the concept was interesting but in application it was cumbersome. In response, others came up with the idea of using steam pressure to force the water through the ground coffee in a filter. This concept was the precursor to the stovetop, Moka-style espresso maker. It also paved the way toward applying this technology to large gas- and electric-powered coffee brewers that would no longer boil the coffee after it had been brewed since the coffee would be extracted directly into the cups.

The development of new methods of brewing a rich, full-bodied cup of coffee seems to have been centered primarily in Italy and to some extent in France and Spain. At the beginning of this century the Italians were at the forefront of creating a brewing method that would allow for the rapid exchange of water through the ground coffee, a process that would retain the essence of the beans without tasting bitter or cooked. The coffee would be made to order using much quicker methods. In Italian, the adjective *espresso* means just that: "made to order on the spot." No one realized back then that this simple adjective, destined to become a noun, would ultimately become the most famous and world-recognized name for coffee. Italian names like Pavoni, Gaggia, Lavazza, and Cimbali soon came to be, and remain today, synonymous with the development of modern espresso-brewing technology.

Electric espresso machines for home use were first introduced in North America in the mid- to late seventies, coinciding with the development and growth of the specialty coffee industry. The machines were received with great acclaim and were very popular. Unfortunately, these early pioneers functioned under the principle of steam and did not have as much pressure as the commercial units found in restaurants. Also, the espresso coffee available in most supermarkets was satisfactory for stovetop, Moka-type coffee but was totally unsuitable for the new espresso machines. Consumers soon became frustrated that they could not make a rich, full-bodied cup of espresso. Furthermore, cappuccino, which was becoming a popular coffee beverage in restaurants, did not seem to come out well at home. The reason for this was that the intense steam needed to froth the milk was just not available if the user did not immediately use the trapped steam left over from heating the water for the espresso. Still, regardless of the obstacles, Americans were hooked and Italians and other European manufacturers continued their efforts to develop a better espresso machine.

In the late 1980s we were finally introduced to the pump espresso machine, probably the most important achievement in home espresso brewing (see cross-section illustration below). Far superior to anything seen before, the pump machines draw small quantities of water from a central container or tank (1) by means of an electrical pump (2). The water is then transferred to a small thermal boiler or heated coils (3), which heat the water for brewing the espresso and producing the steam for frothing milk. Once the water reaches the optimum brewing temperature (190° to 205°F), it is then forced by the pump through the diffuser or brewing head (4) and then through the ground coffee in the filter (5) as it rests in the filter holder (6), and from there into the cups. The pump espresso machines also have two thermostats, one that controls the heat applied to the water for making espresso and one that controls the considerably higher temperature needed for producing a steady supply of intense steam for frothing milk. Available from numerous,

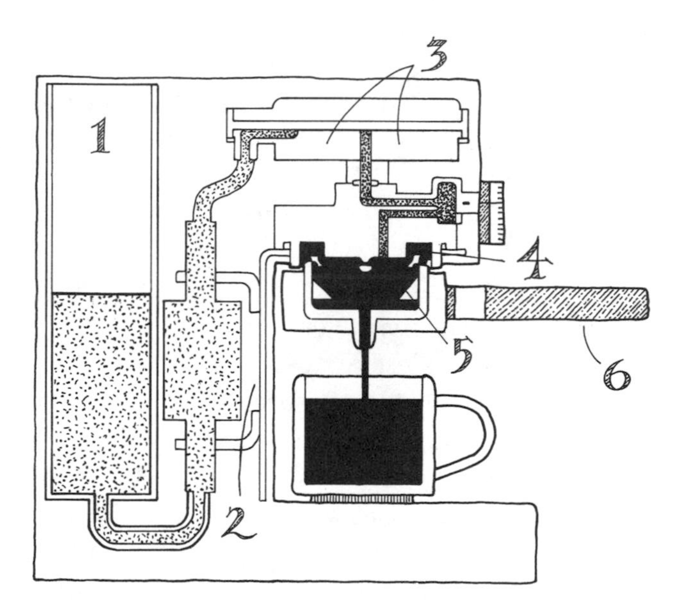

Pump Espresso Machine: (1) tank; (2) pump, (3) boiler; (4) diffuser; (5) filter; (6) filter holder.

highly reputable manufacturers at relatively affordable prices, the quintessential home espresso machine had finally been designed for the home *barista,* or espresso maker.

Using improved technology, the earlier steam espresso machines have also been improved (see cross-section illustration below), even though the espresso they make is still not as intense in flavor and aroma as that made by the pump machines. The boiler, which also acts as the water container (1), is filled with water, and the safety cap (2) is screwed securely in place so the water can be heated under pressure by the heating coils (3). As the water heats it produces steam, which forces the hot water through the diffuser or brewing head (4) and then through the ground coffee in the filter (5) as it rests in the filter holder (6). The espresso brews into the glass container (7) that comes with the appliance. Because of advances in technology, most of the new steam models froth milk just as well as the pump versions, although the steam must be used at once, since it is a by-product of brewing the espresso.

Another type of espresso machine available for home use is the piston espresso

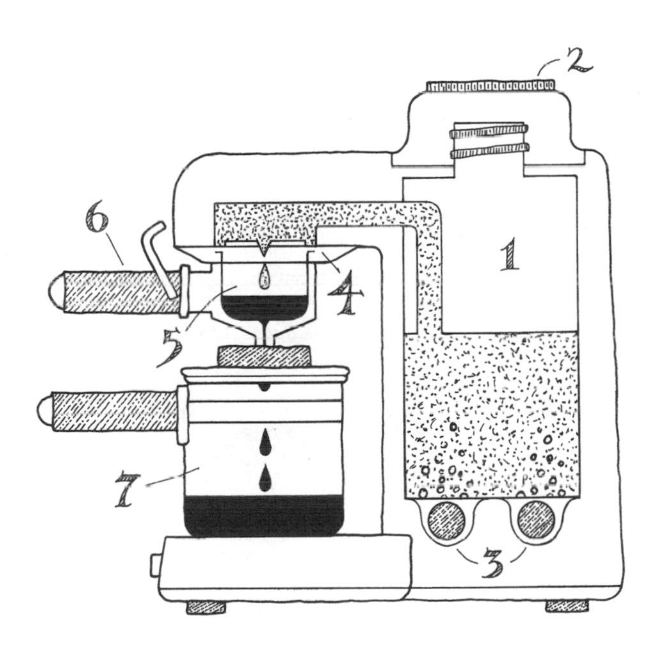

Steam Espresso Machine: (1) boiler; (2) safety cap; (3) heating coils; (4) diffuser; (5) filter; (6) filter holder; (7) glass container.

machine. Marketed under the brand name of La Pavoni, this machine is based on a brewing process developed prior to World War II. This concept is quite simple (see cross-section illustration below). The boiler, which also acts as the water container (1), is filled with water and the safety cap (2) is screwed securely in place so that the water can be heated in the boiler under high pressure. The coffee is then placed in the filter (3), which rests in the filter holder (4) and is locked into position. When the water is hot, the user manually raises the lever (5), which releases the appropriate amount of water from the boiler to make the espresso. As the lever is lowered the espresso is extracted in the cups. Due to the design of the piston espresso machine, the steam from heating the water is contained in the boiler and is drawn off for frothing, as needed.

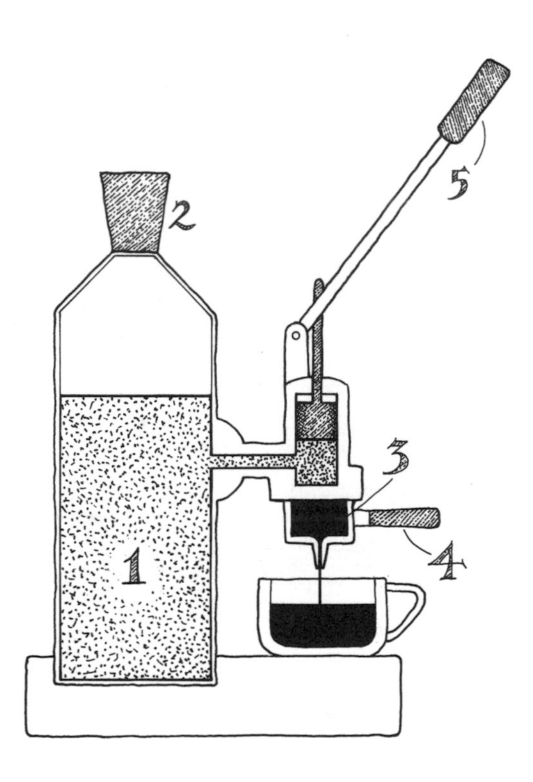

Piston Espresso Machine: (1) boiler; (2) safety cap; (3) filter; (4) filter holder; (5) lever.

MAKING ESPRESSO AT HOME

As specialty coffee sales have increased dramatically in the United States—500 percent over the past twenty years, climbing from 66 million pounds to 33 billion pounds a year—so too has the purchase and use of home espresso machines. A recent joint survey taken by *U.S. News and World Report* and CNN finds that 10 percent, or approximately 8.3 million, American households own an espresso machine and that 43 percent of those, approximately 3.6 million households, use it frequently. That amounts to a lot of espresso. In fact, dollar retail sales of espresso machines increased 21.5 percent in 1994 alone.

The key objective of all espresso machines is to extract 1 to 1½ ounces of espresso in approximately 25 seconds, once the water is hot. A cup of good espresso should have intense aroma, thick cream (or crema), and a full, rich body. The aroma of the espresso is achieved by using the proper grind of good-quality coffee, roasted and blended specifically for espresso. The crema that forms at the top of the espresso is a dense espresso foam that is formed by the dispersion of the oils and air contained in the emulsion. The full-bodied quality of the espresso is due to the presence of tiny drops of oil and very fine particles of ground coffee, which are extracted by the water. Well-made espresso will contain approximately 25 percent of these extracted substances as compared to 16 to 18 percent in a cup of filtered or drip coffee. In order for espresso to be intensely aromatic and full-bodied with a pleasant, persistent aftertaste and a dense, frothy crema, some very simple yet basic steps and practices should be followed. The manufacturers have designed their espresso machines in order to brew the coffee with enough pressure so the espresso achieves the aforementioned qualities. You, the home *barista,* must do your part to ensure that the equipment, water, coffee, cups, and timing are precise and perfectly prepared beforehand.

THE EQUIPMENT

The espresso you are making will only be as good as the espresso machine you are using and the condition in which it is maintained. For the most part, the espresso machines available today for home use make great espresso. They must, however, be maintained properly to assure the best-quality coffee possible. Before using your espresso machine for the first time or after prolonged periods of infrequent use, refer to the owner's manual and instructions that were provided by the manufacturer so that you may properly prime it. By doing so you will also remove any impurities or mineral sediment that may be in the boiler and components, particles that can adversely affect the operation of the appliance and the flavor of the coffee. Usually this requires that you simply flush the brewing diffuser (the part where the water comes in contact with the coffee filter) and the frothing wand with hot water by following a series of steps and operations as indicated in your owner's manual.

The water tank, the diffuser, and the frothing wand should always be kept clean. Never let water sit stagnant in the water tank if you do not plan to use your espresso machine every day. If using a pump unit, empty the tank and wash with a clean cloth and warm soapy water. Rinse well to remove any soap residue and towel dry with a clean kitchen cloth. Any water left in the pump or internal components of the espresso machine will be discharged when the unit is flushed with hot water.

On each occasion you make espresso, after making your last cup you should always clean the diffuser with a damp kitchen cloth or sponge to remove any coffee grounds. The coffee filters and the filter holder must also be cleaned after making the last shot of espresso. You can do this by simply placing them under cold running water to remove any grounds or coffee residue. The spouts in the filter holder should also be checked periodically to make sure that there is no coffee buildup or grounds blocking the openings. The easiest way to clean the spouts is with a pipe cleaner or by soaking the filter holder in warm water.

If you are using a steam espresso machine, always be certain to wash the glass beaker with warm, sudsy water to remove any coffee reside. Rinse well with clean water to remove any soap residue.

In order to froth milk with maximum pressure, you should always wipe off any dry milk residue from the frothing wand or attachment after each use. The small holes located at the end of the frothing wand should also be checked periodically to make sure that they are not clogged. An easy way to do this is to open the steam valve slowly and check to see if steam comes out of the holes, first; if not, unclog the holes with a straight pin.

THE COFFEE

Choosing the right type and grind of coffee for brewing espresso is extremely important. Espresso coffee is readily available in two forms: whole bean and ground. After coffee is roasted and packaged in vacuum-sealed packages or containers it has a shelf life of approximately six months unopened. If buying loose beans that will either be ground by the retailer or at home, always make sure that the beans are fresh. Since oxygen and light rob coffee of its fragrance and flavor, never purchase beans from open bins or from a retailer that has a slow turnover of coffee. Beans

should be fragrant and not oily, nor should they have been allowed to sit out at retail for more than a few days. Preferably, they should either be purchased in small, vacuum-sealed bags or in cans that provide the coffee with an oxygen-free environment until opened.

Once opened, packages of coffee should be stored in airtight opaque containers in a cool dark place. Contrary to popular belief, coffee should not be frozen, for the intense cold can alter its flavor and cause the oils to congeal. Once you have determined the type and brand of coffee you like best and have located a reputable retailer, never purchase more than you plan to use in a week. This way you will be assured a fresh cup of espresso every time.

Ground espresso coffee, with a texture similar to fine table salt, is much finer than drip and filter coffee. It should take no more longer than 25 to 30 seconds to extract a 1½-ounce shot of espresso with crema. If the coffee is ground too coarsely the water will flow too quickly, the espresso will be underextracted, and you will not be able to capture all of the characteristics of the blend. If the coffee is too fine the water will have a difficult time penetrating the coffee, the espresso will be overextracted, and it will be too thick and concentrated in flavor; it may even have a burnt taste, since the grounds will become overheated from long contact with the hot diffuser.

Most espresso machines come with two filters—a small one to make one 1 to 1½-ounce cup or shot of espresso and a larger filter to make two shots or cups. They also come with a spoon for measuring approximately 1 tablespoon of ground coffee for each shot or cup of espresso. Always use the proper amount of coffee for the number of shots or cups that you are making. Do not over- or underfill the filters, since you will encounter the same problems that arise when using the wrong grind of coffee.

Most espresso machines come with a tamper, a plastic tool with a round flat bottom that allows you to tamp, or pack, the ground coffee into the filter. By tamping the coffee you are pushing it down so it does not come into direct contact with the diffuser. Tamped coffee also offers resistance to the water as it flows through, adding to the extracted essence of the brew and assisting in the creation of the crema. After measuring the coffee and placing it in the filter, apply even pressure on the coffee with the tamper. This is extremely important so that the coffee lies evenly in the filter and allows the espresso to flow evenly and simultaneously through the two spouts of the filter holder. By applying even pressure, the water will encounter just the right amount of resistance and the espresso will flow, as they say in Italian, *come la coda del topo* (like the tail of a mouse)—thin and even. A few espresso machines even have the unique feature of automatic tamping. The user has only to measure the coffee into the filter holder and lock the holder into position. The coffee is automatically tamped by the appliance. Check with the owner's manual of your specific machine to determine the exact type of operation.

COFFEE GRINDERS

The easiest way to make espresso, or any coffee for that matter, is to purchase ground coffee. If you wish to grind your own beans you have a few options to choose from: hand-held manual grinders, electric burr grinders, and electric blade grinders.

The oldest method of grinding coffee beans is with a hand-held manual coffee grinder. The beans are placed in the grinder and the handle is turned, rotating a series of stones or wheels that grind the coffee to the desired texture with the ground coffee usually falling into a bottom or front trapdoor. An adjusting nut allows for an infinite selection of grinds.

An electric burr grinder is similar to the hand-held type. Burr grinders usually have a preset number of grind settings, which makes it easier to choose the appropriate grind desired. Still, they are much more expensive, costing approximately $200 to $250, compared to $40 to $50 for a very good hand-held manual grinder.

Another option in coffee grinders is the electric blade grinder, which chops the coffee into small pieces. While low cost makes these the most commonly sold grinder (from $20 to $50), they also do the worst job of grinding. Since the beans are being chopped, there is less consistency to the grind. I have, however, found one that seems to work better than the others—the Bosch MKM6.

If you plan to grind your own coffee, it is essential to maintain your grinder in a very clean state if you want to keep the freshly ground coffee from mixing with stale, perhaps rancid coffee. Only grind enough coffee for immediate use. When done grinding, always shake out the machine to remove any remaining coffee particles. If possible, wipe out the grinding chamber with a clean kitchen cloth to remove the oils and any remaining coffee dust and particles.

FLAVORED COFFEE

Flavored coffees have become very popular. Purists, however, scoff at these, and this is one instance in which I agree with them. For the most part, flavored coffees use inferior grades of coffee beans that have been sprayed with flavored oils to mask the true mediocrity of their taste. They are also usually more expensive. If you wish to drink flavored espresso and coffee beverages, I suggest you try using some of the excellent espresso syrups and flavorings available at most specialty coffee and food stores. For more information on these, please see page 55.

WATER

Since water comprises over 95 percent of a cup of espresso, you should always make sure that you are using fresh, room temperature water when brewing espresso. If you live in an area where the water is hard, you should consider using filtered water to cut down on the amount of minerals. Mineral deposit buildup can also quickly cause the demise of your espresso machine, and can mask the true flavor of the espresso as well.

CUPS

Traditionally, espresso is served in small (2-ounce), heavy ceramic cups, also known as demitasses. One big mistake people usually make is not preheating the cups before brewing the espresso. In coffee bars, cafés, and restaurants, the cups are usually stored on top of the espresso machines, where they are warmed from the heat of the boiler. Since the water used to brew espresso is not as hot as that used in drip and filter-type coffee makers, espresso brewed into a cold cup will cool quickly as the heat of the espresso is transferred to the cup. A simple and easy way to overcome this is to pour boiling water into the cups before brewing. You can also warm the cups, half filled with water, for 30 to 60 seconds in a microwave oven. When you are ready to brew the espresso, simply pour the hot water out of the cups and dry them with a clean kitchen cloth.

As for cappuccino, traditionally it is not the 16-ounce espresso-milk combo sold in many coffee bars in the United States. An authentic Italian cappuccino is a 1-ounce *caffè ristretto* with 4 ounces (1/2 cup) of frothed milk (page 52). Cappuccino should be made and served in a 6-ounce cappuccino or regular coffee cup, warmed the same way as described for espresso.

THE INSIDER'S GUIDE TO PERFECT ESPRESSO AND CAPPUCCINO

As you have seen, making a perfect cup of espresso is not really that difficult. The following is a step-by-step guide on how to achieve perfect results every time.

1. Fill the water tank or boiler with fresh, room-temperature water. Turn on the espresso machine to begin heating the water.
2. Warm the demitasse or cappuccino cups.
3. Measure the ground coffee and place in the filter. Do not over- or underfill.
4. Tamp down the coffee evenly, with moderate pressure. If any coffee has fallen on top of the filter holder, wipe it off with the palm of your hand so it does not fall into the cup.
5. Position the filter holder under the diffuser and lock it in place.
6. Place the preheated cup or cups under the filter holder spouts. When making one shot or cup of espresso, position the cup so that it sits perfectly under the two spouts, allowing the espresso to flow into the cup. If brewing two cups of espresso, use the large coffee filter and position each cup under a spout.
7. Following the manufacturer's operating instructions, begin brewing the espresso. Since you only want to extract approximately 1½ ounces of espresso, you must be certain not to allow too much water to come in contact with the coffee and flow through the filter. A rule of thumb is to flip on the brewing switch. Once the espresso starts to flow through the filter and into the cup or cups, begin counting to five. At that point, turn off the brewing switch. The remaining extraction should only be the crema. If coffee continues to flow into the cups, remove immediately from under the spouts. From start to finish it should take only 25 to 30 seconds to extract a shot of espresso. If the brewing time is longer, the espresso may have a sharp, bitter taste with very little crema.

THE ALL-ELUSIVE CREMA

While you will most likely be able to make a good cup of espresso each time, achieving perfect crema may be a bit more difficult at first. Crema is the golden-brown espresso cream that forms a head on top of the brewed espresso. Made up of dispersed coffee oils and air, crema adds smooth, rounder flavor to the espresso. The crema should be thick enough to support the weight of a teaspoon of sugar. Due to advances in technology, many espresso machines now have special built-in devices and components that help the formation of crema. In the event you are unable to create perfect crema, please consult the troubleshooting section of this book for practical suggestions and solutions.

FROTHED AND STEAMED MILK

Cappuccino, that wonderful Italian espresso beverage consisting of 1 ounce of espresso and 4 ounces of warm, frothed milk, is even more popular in this country than espresso. Years ago, when the first espresso machines were introduced for home use, many people were discouraged that they could not get the milk to froth properly for cappuccino. Fortunately for us, many manufacturers have improved the frothing capability and capacity of the machines. In fact, some models have special aerators on the frothing wands or frothing devices that make frothing a breeze. Regardless of the machine you own, the following suggestions may assist you.

There are many schools of thought as to the type of milk to use for best results. Since my own household drinks only 1 percent fat milk, that's the milk I always use, and with good results. After trying whole milk, reduced-fat, and no-fat (skim) milk, I will honestly admit that I did not see much of a difference, which I can only attribute to the new and improved frothing devices on the different machines. The choice of the type of milk, then, is yours, although I do not recommend cream, since it is too heavy to froth properly.

The temperature of the milk in cappuccino can cause difficulty for Americans, who like their coffee steaming hot. When frothing milk, however, the hotter it becomes the closer it gets to boiling, and the less froth you will get. So there must be a compromise. If you insist upon very hot coffee, then stick with a latte (page 50) made with hot, steamed milk. If you want to enjoy a true cappuccino, learn to enjoy it warm as the Italians do.

For the best results in frothing, start with cold milk. Special stainless-steel frothing pitchers do the best job, especially the ones that are wider at the bottom than at the top and small enough to fit under the frothing wand of your espresso machine. An 8-ounce pitcher is generally a good size to use. Never use glass pitchers (unless they are Pyrex or other tempered glass), because they can crack from the heat of the steam.

Since the pump and piston espresso machines being sold today produce a steady, constant level of steam and pressure, it does not make a difference whether you froth or steam the milk before or after brewing the espresso. Check the owner's manual for your particular model to verify whether the manufacturer recommends a certain sequence to follow. If none is specified, I suggest that you first brew the espresso and then prepare the milk. When using a steam espresso machine, you must always brew the espresso first before frothing or steaming. If your espresso machine has a special frothing attachment or device, follow those instructions provided by the manufacturer.

To Froth and Steam Milk

To froth milk: Place the wand halfway into the milk and open the valve or switch to release the steam. As bubbles begin to appear and the froth begins to rise, very slowly lower the pitcher so that the tip of the wand approaches the surface of the milk. As you do this the steam forces the milk to increase in volume. The milk is sufficiently frothed when it has many tiny bubbles that just barely form soft peaks and the pitcher is starting to become warm to the touch. The entire process should only take approximately 15 to 25 seconds. The final volume of the frothed milk will be about twice that of the cold milk.

To steam milk: Place the tip of the wand into the milk, almost to the bottom of the pitcher, and open the valve or switch. Allow the milk to heat up until the pitcher is hot to the touch, taking care not to scald the milk. Steamed milk will only thicken and increase in volume slightly and will have little or no froth.

When you are ready to froth or steam, prepare the espresso machine in accordance with the manufacturer's instructions. Place a small heatproof container under the frothing wand or attachment and open the valve or switch. Clear and remove any water condensation and close the valve or switch when steam begins to appear.

Fill the frothing pitcher at least half full with cold milk, bearing in mind that frothed milk will almost double in volume, while steamed milk will only increase by approximately 20 to 25 percent. Holding the pitcher by the handle, place the frothing wand into the cold milk. It may be necessary to tilt the pitcher slightly so that the wand fits.

When the milk has been sufficiently frothed or steamed, shut off the switch or close the valve. Remove the pitcher and proceed with the instructions given in the recipe. The recipes also provide the exact amount of frothed or steamed milk required for the drink that you are preparing as well as the appropriate size cup or glass to use. Never reheat frothed or steamed milk, since milk that has been previously heated will not froth well.

Wipe off the frothing wand with a clean, damp kitchen cloth and turn the steam on for a few seconds to clear out any milk residue.

HELP IS BUT A PHONE CALL AWAY

Some espresso machines come with instructional videos, which can be extremely useful. Use the video as a visual guide as to how brewed espresso and frothed milk should appear. Get to know your espresso machine by carefully reading the owner's manual and any other printed materials provided by the manufacturer. Be willing to experiment with different brands and grinds of coffee until you find the one that works the best with your particular model and that meets your taste preferences. Even if your espresso does not have a perfect head of crema, it will probably taste fine anyway. Also, do not forget that the best source of information on how to use your espresso machine is the manufacturer. All the manufacturers have fully staffed customer service departments with trained representatives who are happy to answer any questions.

ESPRESSO: DISPELLING THE MISCONCEPTIONS

While espresso has been enjoyed in Italy and parts of Europe since the beginning of the century, for the most part it is a relatively new beverage for most Americans.

Over the years, there have been many misconceptions about espresso, probably the most serious of which is that espresso is higher in caffeine than drip or filtered coffee, since, unfortunately, many people confuse intense flavor with high caffeine content. In truth, the caffeine content of a blend or brand is determined by the variety and origin of the coffee beans and not the roast, which, in fact, may even slightly reduce the natural caffeine content of the bean. Much of the world's coffee, be it for espresso or drip coffee (there is no such thing as an espresso coffee variety), is roasted and blended using either arabica, robusta, or a blend of the two. Arabica, which accounts for at least 70 to 100 percent of most espresso blends, contains on average 1.2 percent caffeine, while robusta contains approximately 2.2 percent.

The caffeine content of a cup of coffee also increases dramatically according to the method used to brew it. When the coffee is in direct contact with the water for a longer period of time, the level of caffeine is significantly higher. This is especially true with coffee made using a French press or the drip method. One to 1½ ounces of espresso contains approximately 40 to 90 milligrams of caffeine, depending on the blend, as compared to 110 milligrams in an 8-ounce cup of filtered coffee. Since the human body can absorb and process 150 to 200 milligrams of caffeine an hour, those who are not suffering from any form of hypertension or heart disease can easily enjoy three to four shots of espresso a day. In fact, since caffeine acts as a stimulant on our neuromuscular functions, some claim that it can increase awareness and boost energy levels. Perhaps the Renaissance physician Paracelsus put it best: "Nothing in itself is poison or cure, everything depends on the dosage." Nevertheless, good-quality decaffeinated espresso coffee, available in both beans and ground, can easily be found at retail.

Another misconception about espresso is that those cultures traditionally associated with it drink more coffee than the others who are not. Contrary to popular belief, however, Italians are not the largest consumers of coffee, nor are Americans. Scandinavia, especially Finland (25.5 pounds per person) and Sweden (24.5 pounds per person), is where coffee consumption is the highest in the world. Italy currently ranks number eleven, with coffee consumption at 9.75 pounds a year, while the United States is number ten, with consumption at 10 pounds per person. Nevertheless, the United States is the largest importer of coffee, bringing in an average of 18.1 million sacks or approximately 1.1 million tons of coffee a year.

TAKING IT TO THE NEXT STEP

In addition to preparing delicious, rich cups of espresso and cappuccino with your espresso machine, you can also prepare an endless variety of espresso-based beverages by varying the ratio of coffee to milk or by adding different spirits for after-dinner drinks. In doing my research for this book, I also encountered many interesting classic dessert recipes that use strong coffee as a flavoring ingredient.

The following sections of this book are dedicated to increasing the use of your espresso machine. For the most part, the recipes are simple to prepare and fall into a wide variety of categories, from everyday beverages and desserts to those for special occasions. And for those who are watching their intake of fat and calories, a complete nutritional analysis is provided for each drink and dessert. The nutritional analyses for the espresso drinks with milk are based on using milk with a fat content of 1 percent, and do not include any of the optional accompaniments such as sugar, cinnamon, and so forth unless specified in the recipe.

PART ONE

ESPRESSO AND ESPRESSO DRINKS

HOT ESPRESSO AND MILK DRINKS

The basic espresso recipes contained in this section appear throughout this book as the basis for a variety of espresso drinks and as an ingredient when making desserts and sweets.

You will be introduced to the different types of espresso served in Italy and around the world, drinks that appeal to a wide range of taste preferences. By adding smaller or larger quantities of milk you will learn how to prepare popular espresso drinks like cappuccino, latte, and café au lait with as much finesse as the most experienced *barista*. Most of all, however, you will learn how to experience the ritual of espresso as it is enjoyed in Italy.

ESPRESSO AND VARIATIONS

In addition to a plain shot of espresso, there are three basic variations you can enjoy: Caffè Ristretto (or corto), Caffè Lungo, and Doppio Espresso. As with espresso, they can either be enjoyed straight with sugar on the side or combined with frothed or steamed milk and/or other ingredients to prepare an endless variety of espresso drinks.

Espresso

Traditionally, espresso is brewed using approximately 1 to 1½ tablespoons (1 scoop) of ground espresso coffee and drunk in portions of 1½ ounces. In Italy it is simply served black with sugar on the side. In the United States espresso often appears with a piece of lemon peel in the saucer, which is to be rubbed on the cup's rim for flavor. This custom has been widely practiced by Italian-Americans for years and a theory on its origin is that it was brought back to the U.S. by American GIs after World War II. During the American occupation of Italy, soap and other basic necessities were expensive or unobtainable. In order to sanitize cups and glasses, Italian cafés were rumored to have rubbed the edges with the readily available lemon. The GIs may have thought that the lemon flavor was intentional and continued the practice on their return home. Personally, I find that the lemon peel distracts and takes away from the pleasure of the essence of the coffee on the palate.

1 SERVING

APPROXIMATE NUTRITIONAL ANALYSIS PER 1½-OUNCE SERVING:

0 calories, 0g total fat, 0g saturated fat, 0mg cholesterol, 1mg sodium, 0g carbohydrates, 0g protein

Espresso: the ultimate expression of refined living.

—LUIGI LAVAZZA

Caffè Ristretto

If you desire a stronger cup of espresso, let the cup fill with only 1 ounce of espresso and crema. You have now prepared a caffè ristretto or corto.

1 SERVING

APPROXIMATE NUTRITIONAL ANALYSIS PER 1-OUNCE SERVING:

0 calories, 0g total fat, 0g saturated fat, 0mg cholesterol, 1mg sodium, 0g carbohydrates, 0g protein

Caffè Lungo

If you wish to make a weaker cup of espresso, let the espresso brew longer so that more water flows through the 1 to ½ tablespoons of espresso coffee, producing approximately 3 to 4 ounces of espresso. This is called a caffè lungo or americano. When making a caffè lungo you may need to use a larger cup, preferably a cappuccino or standard-size coffee cup.

1 SERVING

APPROXIMATE NUTRITIONAL ANALYSIS PER 3-OUNCE SERVING:

0 calories, 0g total fat, 0g saturated fat, 0mg cholesterol, 3mg sodium, 0g carbohydrates, 0g protein

Black as the Devil,
Hot as Hell,
Pure as an Angel,
Sweet as Love.

—CHARLES MAURICE DE TALLEYRAND-PÉRIGORD

Doppio Espresso

For those of us who never seem to get enough of a good thing, there is the doppio espresso, or double espresso. Prepare the espresso as if you were going to make two cups, using a heaping scoop of ground coffee (approximately 2 to 3 tablespoons of ground espresso coffee) and the larger of the two filters. Rather than place two cups under the filter holder, use just one larger cup, like that for cappuccino, or a standard-size coffee cup. Let the warmed cup fill with a double shot of 3 to 4 ounces of espresso. Some machines have a standard filter incorporated into the filter holder; if this is the case, fill it as if you were making 2 cups of espresso and not one.

1 SERVING

APPROXIMATE NUTRITIONAL ANALYSIS PER 3-OUNCE SERVING:

0 calories, 0g total fat, 0g saturated fat, 0mg cholesterol, 3mg sodium, 0g carbohydrates, 0g protein

Caffè Macchiato

Caffè macchiato is the first Italian derivation of basic espresso. *Macchiato,* which means "stained" in Italian, is exactly how this classic espresso drink looks when a dollop of frothed milk is added on top of the hot brewed espresso. The small addition of milk does little to change the flavor of the espresso, although for some it may taste smoother.

1 Espresso ($1\frac{1}{2}$ ounces, page 45)
1 heaping tablespoon frothed milk (page 38)

Brew the espresso into a warmed 2-ounce espresso or demitasse cup. Following the frothing instructions given on page 38, froth the milk so that it has many tiny bubbles that barely form soft peaks. Spoon the frothed milk on top of the espresso. Serve with sugar, if desired.

1 SERVING

APPROXIMATE NUTRITIONAL ANALYSIS PER SERVING:

7 calories, 0g total fat, 0g saturated fat, 1mg cholesterol, 9mg sodium, 1g carbohydrates, 1g protein

Caffè Latte

Ordering a latte in the United States is as common as ordering an espresso in Italy. Italians, for the most part, enjoy caffè latte at home for breakfast to accompany their plain breakfast biscuits (slightly sweetened cookies) and slices of bread with butter or jam. Caffè latte is not as strong as cappuccino or café au lait and will be enjoyed by those who prefer more of a milk flavor than a strong espresso taste. Nevertheless, if you are looking to make a latte similar to what you've been enjoying at your local espresso bar, this is not the recipe for you. Check out the one on the next page for Latte Macchiato.

1 Espresso (1½ ounces, page 45)
5 ounces (scant ⅔ cup) steamed milk (page 38)

Brew the espresso into a warmed 2-ounce espresso or standard coffee cup. Following the steaming instructions given on page 38, froth the milk so that it thickens slightly with tiny bubbles. Pour the brewed espresso and steamed milk simultaneously into a warmed French coffee bowl, mug, or tall glass. Serve with sugar, if desired.

1 SERVING

APPROXIMATE NUTRITIONAL ANALYSIS PER SERVING:

64 calories, 2g total fat, 1g saturated fat, 6mg cholesterol, 78mg sodium, 7g carbohydrates, 5g protein

The conversation flowed between them, warm
and refreshing, like a good cup of coffee.

—ROSAMOND LEHMANN,
THE TIME OF LOVE

Latte Macchiato

As you have seen from the previous recipe, an authentic Italian caffè latte is not as large as an American latte. An American latte, which can contain up to 16 ounces of frothed milk, in Italy is called a latte macchiato, which literally means "stained milk." As with caffè latte, latte macchiato is an Italian breakfast drink, although in this country it is enjoyed all day long. The following recipe uses 8 ounces (1 cup) of milk. The quantities can be doubled, if desired.

1 Espresso ($1\frac{1}{2}$ ounces, page 45)
8 ounces (1 cup) steamed milk,
with little or no froth (page 38)

Brew the espresso into a warmed 2-ounce espresso or demitasse cup. Following the steaming instructions given on page 38, steam the milk so that it thickens slightly with tiny bubbles. Pour the brewed espresso and steamed milk simultaneously into a warmed French coffee bowl, large mug, or tall glass. Serve with sugar, if desired.

1 SERVING

APPROXIMATE NUTRITIONAL ANALYSIS PER SERVING:

102 calories, 3g total fat, 2g saturated fat, 10mg cholesterol, 124mg sodium, 12g carbohydrates, 8g protein

CAPPUCCINO

Cappuccino is probably the best known of Italian coffee beverages. It is named after the Capuchin friars, a Catholic religious order, whose hooded robes resemble the color of this beverage.

1 Caffè Ristretto (1 ounce, page 46)
4 ounces (1/2 cup) frothed milk (page 38)
Granulated sugar (optional)
Ground cinnamon or unsweetened cocoa powder (optional)

Brew the caffè ristretto into a warmed 6-ounce cappuccino or standard coffee cup. Following the frothing instructions given on page 38, froth the milk so that it has many tiny bubbles that barely form soft peaks. Pour the frothed milk into the cup. The foam should form a white oval in the center of the cup surrounded by a golden ring of crema. Sweeten with sugar and sprinkle with cinnamon or unsweetened cocoa powder, if desired.

1 SERVING

APPROXIMATE NUTRITIONAL ANALYSIS PER SERVING:

51 calories, 1g total fat, 1g saturated fat, 5mg cholesterol, 63mg sodium, 6g carbohydrates, 4g protein

CAFÉ AU LAIT

The classic French beverage for breakfast, café au lait and its variations are enjoyed throughout most of the Mediterranean as the drink of choice in the morning.

1 Caffè Lungo (3 ounces, page 47)
4 ounces frothed milk (page 38)
Granulated sugar (optional)

Brew the caffè lungo into a warmed 6-ounce cappuccino or standard coffee cup. Following the frothing instructions given on page 38, froth the milk so that it has many tiny bubbles that barely form soft peaks. Pour the brewed espresso and frothed milk simultaneously into a warmed French coffee bowl or a large mug. Serve with sugar, if desired.

1 SERVING

APPROXIMATE NUTRITIONAL ANALYSIS PER SERVING:

51 calories, 1g total fat, 1g saturated fat, 5mg cholesterol, 65mg sodium, 6g carbohydrates, 4g protein

The morning cup of coffee has an exhilaration about it which the cheering influence of the afternoon or evening cup of tea cannot be expected to reproduce.

—OLIVER WENDELL HOLMES, SR.

CAFFÈ BREVE

Even though *caffè breve* means "short coffee" in Italian, do not try to order one in Italy since the *barista* will have no idea what you are asking for. As with many of the popular espresso drinks in this country, caffè breve is the creation of a Seattle, not an Italian, *barista.* Regardless of its origin, the frothed half-and-half of the breve makes for extra smoothness.

1 Caffè Ristretto (1 ounce, page 46)
4 ounces (1/2 cup) frothed half-and-half (page 38)
Granulated sugar (optional)
Ground cinnamon or unsweetened cocoa powder (optional)

Brew the caffè ristretto into a warmed 6-ounce cappuccino or standard coffee cup. Following the frothing instructions on page 38, froth the half-and-half so that it has many tiny bubbles that barely form soft peaks. Pour the frothed half-and-half into the cup. The foam should form a white oval in the center of the cup surrounded by a golden ring of crema. Sweeten with sugar and sprinkle with cinnamon or unsweetened cocoa, if desired.

1 SERVING

APPROXIMATE NUTRITIONAL ANALYSIS PER SERVING:

158 calories, 14g total fat, 9g saturated fat, 45mg cholesterol, 50mg sodium, 5g carbohydrates, 4g protein

Flavored Espresso, Latte, and Cappuccino

As the coffee culture has grown in popularity in North America so has the appearance of flavored coffee beans and syrups. While there are some very good-quality flavored beans on the market, for the most part the quality of the coffee is inferior to traditional blends and roasts (page 32). For those individuals interested in adding different and exotic flavors to their espresso and espresso drinks, a wide variety of flavored syrups is available at most coffee and specialty food stores. These Italian-style syrups, available in traditional flavors like hazelnut and almond, were originally used to flavor seltzer for soft drinks. They are now also available in a wide variety of fruit and blended flavors. When using syrups, always choose one that will complement the flavor of the beverage and not mask the flavor of the espresso. As with almost anything you buy, the more natural the syrup, the better the flavor.

The following are some guidelines for using flavored syrups.

Espresso: For each 1½ ounces of espresso add 1 teaspoon of flavored syrup, or to taste.

Cappuccino, Lattes, and Café au Lait: For each 5- to 6-ounce serving add 1 to 2 teaspoons of flavored syrup, or to taste.

Caffè Mocha

Once coffeehouses began to pop up throughout Europe, the proprietors were soon busy developing new espresso drinks to serve their clientele. The following is a version of one such drink that was popular in Italian cafés up until the last world war.

1 Espresso (1½ ounces, page 45)
4 ounces (½ cup) frothed milk (page 38)
1 teaspoon unsweetened cocoa powder
Granulated sugar (optional)

Brew the espresso into a warmed 2-ounce espresso or demitasse cup. Pour the espresso into a warmed tall mug or glass. Following the frothing instructions given on page 38, froth the milk so that it has many tiny bubbles that barely form soft peaks. Add the cocoa powder to half the frothed milk. Stir well to blend. Pour on top of the espresso. Do not stir. Top with remaining frothed milk. Serve with sugar, if desired.

1 SERVING

APPROXIMATE NUTRITIONAL ANALYSIS PER SERVING:

55 calories, 2g total fat, 1g saturated fat, 5mg cholesterol, 63mg sodium, 7g carbohydrates, 4g protein

Hot Chocolate

The frothing wand of the espresso machine can also be used for preparing hot milk drinks that do not contain espresso. Hot chocolate made with frothed milk is what hot chocolate is all about. Chocolate, the imperial drink of the Aztecs, was and continues to be traditionally made in parts of Central and South America using a *molinillo,* a wooden utensil placed in the chocolate pot and rotated between the palms of the hands, aerating the warming mixture and producing a thick yet light drink. You can achieve the same delicious results by using the frothing wand of the espresso machine.

8 ounces (1 cup) milk
1 teaspoon unsweetened cocoa powder
2 teaspoons granulated sugar

Following the frothing instructions given on page 38, froth the milk just until the frothing pitcher begins to feel warm. Stir in the cocoa powder and sugar. Continue frothing until the hot chocolate has many tiny bubbles and just begins to form soft peaks.

1 SERVING

APPROXIMATE NUTRITIONAL ANALYSIS PER SERVING:

138 calories, 3g total fat, 2g saturated fat, 10mg cholesterol, 123mg sodium, 8g carbohydrates, 4g protein

Eggnog Latte

Another of the many Seattle espresso culture creations, eggnog latte makes a great breakfast in a glass for those on the run.

1 large egg yolk
2 tablespoons granulated sugar
4 ounces (1/2 cup) milk
1 tablespoon brandy (optional)
Grated nutmeg

In a small bowl, beat together the egg yolk and sugar until smooth. Add the milk and whisk to blend. Pour through a small mesh strainer into the frothing pitcher to filter out any large particles. Following the frothing instructions given on page 38, froth the mixture so that it has many tiny bubbles that barely form soft peaks. Continue frothing until the mixture reaches 160°F on an instant-read thermometer (see note). Pour the frothed eggnog latte into a warmed 6-ounce cappuccino or standard coffee cup. Stir in the brandy, if desired. Sprinkle with grated nutmeg.

Note: The 160°F temperature is necessary for avoiding the risk of salmonella from the egg yolk.

1 SERVING

APPROXIMATE NUTRITIONAL ANALYSIS PER SERVING:

210 calories, 7g total fat, 3g saturated fat, 217mg cholesterol, 69mg sodium, 31g carbohydrates, 7g protein

Spirited Espresso and Milk Drinks

Coffee drinks with a shot or two of spirits have been enjoyed around the world for centuries. Early Swedish coffee drinkers found that a shot of brandy or schnapps in their morning coffee helped fortify them to endure the Arctic cold and to perhaps ward off the risk of an upset stomach. Their beloved *kaffegök,* or "cuckoo coffee," derives its name from the superstition that anyone who heard the first cuckoo bird of spring on an empty stomach would suffer severe indigestion. Obviously, these wise Scandinavians believed that coffee and spirits would protect them from the power of the infamous cuckoo, not just in spring, but all year.

In Spain and Portugal, old-timers still have their morning *café con leche* (coffee and hot milk) along with a shot of *anís* or *coñac* on the side to *matar el gusanillo* (kill the worm) or as they say in Portuguese, *matar el bicho* (kill the bug). You see, the inhabitants of the Iberian Peninsula are also concerned with their stomachs, believing that a shot of spirits along with their coffee will kill off any intestinal parasites, or for that matter, whatever may be ailing you.

Today, for the most part, spirited espresso and coffee drinks are enjoyed after a special dinner or a long day out in the cold. The following selection of drinks provides an international perspective on taking espresso to the next level of enjoyment.

Torino Espresso

A prize-winning combination of espresso and spirits honoring the ancient Italian city of Turin.

1 strip lemon zest
1 whole clove
1 Caffè Ristretto
  (1 ounce, page 46)
1 ounce brandy
1 ounce dark rum
Granulated sugar (optional)

Twist the lemon zest and drop it, along with the clove, into a warmed 6-ounce cappuccino or standard coffee cup. Brew the caffè ristretto into the cup. Add the brandy and rum. Stir to blend. Serve with sugar, if desired.

1 SERVING

APPROXIMATE NUTRITIONAL ANALYSIS PER SERVING:

129 calories, 0g total fat, 0g saturated fat, 0mg cholesterol, 2mg sodium, 0g carbohydrates, 0g protein

Here's your coffee, sir. . . . It doesn't take much to make it: put in the right measure and don't spill it on the flame. Let the froth rise, then quickly turn it down.

—CARLO GOLDONI,
THE PERSIAN BRIDE

Espresso Veneziano

Over the course of time it becomes difficult, if not impossible, to reconstruct the origin of foods and beverages. One can only assume that the addition of whipped cream by the Venetians to the classic Italian caffè corretto was an influence that arrived from nearby Vienna.

1 Caffè Lungo (4 ounces, page 47)
1 ounce brandy
1 teaspoon granulated sugar
Soft whipped cream

Brew the caffè lungo into a warmed 6-ounce cappuccino or standard coffee cup. Add the brandy and sugar. Stir to blend. Top with a large dollop of whipped cream.

1 SERVING

APPROXIMATE NUTRITIONAL ANALYSIS PER SERVING:

119 calories, 4g total fat, 3g saturated fat, 15mg cholesterol, 8mg sodium, 5g carbohydrates, 1g protein

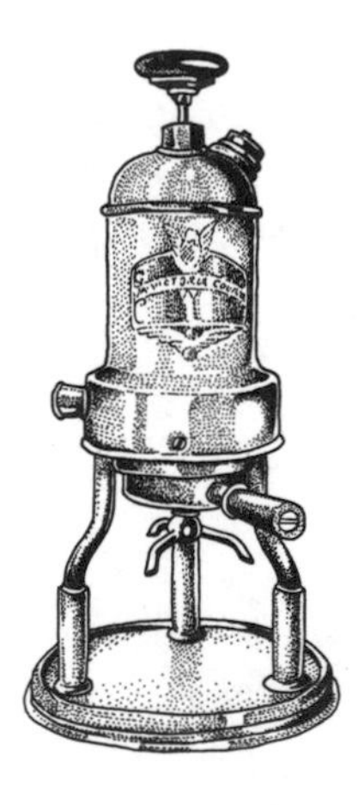

Espresso Gloria

The following recipe is a variation of classic Coffee Gloria, which is made with coffee and brandy. The same recipe without the brown sugar would be an Italian *caffè corretto,* or as we would say in English, a spiked coffee.

1 Caffè Lungo (4 ounces, page 47)
1 ounce brandy
1 teaspoon light brown sugar, packed

Brew the caffè lungo into a warmed 6-ounce cappuccino or standard coffee cup. Stir in the brandy and sugar.

1 SERVING

APPROXIMATE NUTRITIONAL ANALYSIS PER SERVING:

76 calories, 0g total fat, 0g saturated fat, 0mg cholesterol, 4mg sodium, 3g carbohydrates, 0g protein

Espresso Incontro

Chocolate and coffee complement the flavor of each when blended together in desserts and beverages. Espresso incontro is a prime example.

1 Doppio Espresso
(3 ounces, page 48)
1 ounce dark rum
1 teaspoon crème de cacao
Granulated sugar (optional)

Brew the espresso into a warmed 6-ounce cappuccino or standard coffee cup. Add the rum and crème de cacao. Serve with sugar, if desired.

1 SERVING

APPROXIMATE NUTRITIONAL ANALYSIS PER SERVING:

84 calories, 0g total fat, 0g saturated fat, 0mg cholesterol, 4mg sodium, 3g carbohydrates, 0g protein

The best maxim I know in life, is to drink your coffee when you can, and when you cannot, to be easy without it.

—JONATHAN SWIFT

(facing) Tiramisù with a cup of Espresso

(above) Espresso Crème Brûlée with a cup of Espresso Brûlot

(facing) Coffee Parfait with a glass of Iced Espresso

Mocha Biscotti, Mocha Frappé, Chocolate-Covered Espresso Beans,
Mocha Truffles, Coffee and Milk Caramels, and Irish Espresso

Mocha Mint Chocolate-Chip Cookies with a glass of San Francisco Cappuccino

(facing) Swiss Chocolate Log with a cup of Café au Lait

Caffè Nerino

An after-dinner taste treat, the following recipe was adapted from a recipe provided to me by Lavazza Premium Coffees.

1 Espresso (1 ½ ounces, page 45)
1 ounce Cointreau
1 ounce brandy
1½ teaspoons cream of coconut
Unsweetened cocoa powder

Brew the espresso into a warmed 6-ounce cappuccino or standard coffee cup. Stir in the Cointreau, brandy, and cream of coconut. Sprinkle with cocoa powder to taste.

1 SERVING

APPROXIMATE NUTRITIONAL ANALYSIS PER SERVING:

207 calories, 3g total fat, 3g saturated fat, 0mg cholesterol, 5mg sodium, 17g carbohydrates, 1g protein

(facing) Coffee Meringues with a cup of Caffè Macchiato

Swiss Entlebucher Coffee

It was our second day in Switzerland, and we had gone to a small village high in the mountains in the Valais with our good friends and hosts. As the sun began to set, it started to become chilly as we sat in the café watching the skiers. Someone decided to order a round of entlebucher coffees, a traditional Swiss coffee drink usually enjoyed after a long day on the slopes. I do not know what impressed me most, the pine twig in the glass of steaming coffee or the heady aroma of the coffee and kirsch. This is, without a doubt, the most appropriate of drinks to be enjoyed sitting around a blazing fire.

- 1 thin, flexible pine twig, longer than the height of the glass
- 2 Caffè Lungo (6 ounces total, page 47)
- 1 ounce kirsch or other eau de vie
- Sugar cubes, optional

Remove any needles from the twig and bend it a couple of times without breaking to release resin. Brew the caffè lungo into a warmed 6-ounce cappuccino or standard coffee cup. Pour into a warmed tall glass containing the pine twig. Add the kirsch. Serve with sugar, if desired. Stir with the pine twig to blend.

1 SERVING

APPROXIMATE NUTRITIONAL ANALYSIS PER SERVING:

90 calories, 0g total fat, 0g saturated fat, 0mg cholesterol, 10mg sodium, 4g carbohydrates, 0g protein

Espresso Grog

A wonderful hot toddy to warm the body and soul on a blustery winter's day or night.

1 teaspoon dark brown sugar, packed
Pinch each of ground cinnamon, nutmeg, and cloves
1 pea-size piece of butter, at room temperature
1 Caffè Lungo (4 ounces, page 47)
1 ounce dark rum
Twist each of lemon and orange zest

Place the sugar, spices, and butter in the bottom of a warmed 6-ounce cappuccino or standard coffee cup. Brew the caffè lungo into the cup. Add the rum and stir to blend. Twist and drop the lemon and orange zest into the grog.

1 SERVING

APPROXIMATE NUTRITIONAL ANALYSIS PER SERVING:

80 calories, 0g total fat, 0g saturated fat, 1mg cholesterol, 5mg sodium, 4g carbohydrates, 0g protein

ESPRESSO BRÛLOT

This traditional coffee drink from New Orleans, flavored with spices, citrus peel, and flaming brandy, provides a dramatic touch to any get-together.

4 Caffè Lungo (12 ounces total, page 47)
6 ounces (3/4 cup) brandy
1 strip orange zest
1 strip lemon zest
5 whole cloves
1 cinnamon stick
4 teaspoons granulated sugar

Brew the caffè lungo and set aside. In a small nonreactive saucepan, combine the brandy, citrus zests, cloves, cinnamon stick, and sugar. Bring to a boil. Lower the heat and simmer 2 minutes. Pour the espresso into four standard coffee cups. Ignite the brandy mixture with a match. When the flame burns out, ladle the brandy over the coffee.

4 SERVINGS

APPROXIMATE NUTRITIONAL ANALYSIS PER SERVING:

113 calories, 0g total fat, 0g saturated fat, 0mg cholesterol, 6mg sodium, 4g carbohydrates, 0g protein

Irish Espresso

It is rumored that Irish coffee, while best made with real Irish whiskey, was first served at the legendary San Franciscan drinking hole, the Buenavista. The addition of espresso rather than the customary brewed coffee adds extra body to this heady drink. Irish coffee is traditionally served in special 6-to 8-ounce glass mugs called Irish coffee glasses.

1 Caffè Lungo
  (4 ounces, page 47)
1 rounded teaspoon granulated
  sugar
1 ounce Irish whiskey
Soft whipped cream

Brew the caffè lungo into a warmed 6-ounce cappuccino or standard coffee cup. Place the sugar in an Irish coffee glass. With spoon in glass, pour in espresso and whiskey. Top with whipped cream.

1 SERVING

APPROXIMATE NUTRITIONAL ANALYSIS PER SERVING:

140 calories, 6g total fat, 3g saturated fat, 20mg cholesterol, 9mg sodium, 5g carbohydrates, 0g protein

Only Irish coffee provides in a single glass all four essential food groups: alcohol, caffeine, sugar, and fat.

—ALEX LEVINE

Russian Coffee

Although tea served with fruit preserves is the national drink of choice in Russia, I believe that the following espresso drink, fortified with good Russian vodka, would get more than one nod of approval from our Russian friends.

- 1 Doppio Espresso (3 ounces, page 48)
- 1 ounce Russian vodka
- $1^1/_2$ tablespoons soft whipped cream
- Granulated sugar (optional)

Brew the espresso into a warmed 6-ounce cappuccino or standard coffee cup. Stir in the vodka and top with whipped cream. Serve with sugar, if desired.

1 SERVING

APPROXIMATE NUTRITIONAL ANALYSIS PER SERVING:

109 calories, 4g total fat, 3g saturated fat, 15mg cholesterol, 8mg sodium, 1g carbohydrates, 0g protein

Coffee: Induces wit. Good only if it comes through Havre. After a big dinner party it is taken standing up. Take it without sugar—very swank: gives the impression you have lived in the East.

—GUSTAVE FLAUBERT

Café à la Polonaise

The following is an award-winning recipe from the Italian Barmen's Association. As with any whipped cream–topped spirited espresso drink, do not mix the drink after you top it with the cream. Sip it through the whipped cream for a real taste treat.

- 1 Doppio Espresso (3 ounces, page 48)
- 1 ounce vodka
- 1 ounce Cointreau
- Soft whipped cream
- ½ teaspoon grated orange zest
- Grated nutmeg
- Granulated sugar (optional)

Brew the espresso into a warmed 6-ounce cappuccino or standard coffee cup. Add the vodka and Cointreau. Stir to blend. Top with whipped cream and sprinkle with grated orange zest and nutmeg. Serve with sugar, if desired.

1 SERVING

APPROXIMATE NUTRITIONAL ANALYSIS PER SERVING:

226 calories, 4g total fat, 3g saturated fat, 15mg cholesterol, 11mg sodium, 17g carbohydrates, 0g protein

CARIBBEAN POUSSE-CAFÉ

Pousse-café literally means "push the coffee" in French and refers to liqueurs and spirits that are served on the side with a cup of after-dinner coffee. This Caribbean version layers, in an attractive glass, different types of tropical-flavored liqueurs, which are then topped off with a head of espresso.

1 ounce each coffee-flavored liqueur, Curaçao, crème de banane, and coconut liqueur (or other tropical fruit-flavored liqueurs of choice)

1 ounce dark rum

1 Doppio Espresso (3 ounces, page 48)

Layer the liqueurs into an Irish coffee glass (a special 6-to 8-ounce glass mug traditionally used to serve Irish coffee) by pouring the heaviest and thickest in first. So as not to upset each of the layers, pour the liqueur over the inverted side of a tablespoon so it trickles down slowly. Finish with a layer of dark rum, poured the same way.

Brew the espresso into a warmed 6-ounce cappuccino or standard coffee cup. Pour slowly over the inverted side of a tablespoon, on top of the rum. Do not stir. Sip through a straw.

1 SERVING

APPROXIMATE NUTRITIONAL ANALYSIS PER SERVING:

465 calories, 0g total fat, 0g saturated fat, 0mg cholesterol, 14mg sodium, 65g carbohydrates, 0g protein

Jamaican Coffee

There are probably as many different variations of Jamaican coffee as there are coffee beans! This version is a personal favorite.

- 1 Caffè Lungo (4 ounces, page 47)
- 1 ounce Espresso Liqueur (page 80) or other coffee-flavored liqueur
- Soft whipped cream
- Ground cinnamon
- Granulated sugar (optional)

Brew the caffè lungo into a warmed 6-ounce cappuccino or standard coffee cup. Stir in the espresso or coffee liqueur. Top with whipped cream and sprinkle with cinnamon. Serve with sugar, if desired.

1 SERVING

APPROXIMATE NUTRITIONAL ANALYSIS PER SERVING:

156 calories, 4g total fat, 3g saturated fat, 15mg cholesterol, 10mg sodium, 17g carbohydrates, 0g protein

Caffè Calypso

Tropical-flavored liqueurs are very popular additions to spirited espresso drinks, as is true with this one, caffè calypso.

1 Caffè Lungo (4 ounces, page 47)
1 ounce Malibu or other coconut-flavored liqueur
1 ounce Espresso Liqueur (page 80) or other coffee-flavored liqueur
2 ounces (1/4 cup) frothed milk (page 38)

Brew the caffè lungo into a warmed 6-ounce cappuccino or standard coffee cup. Add the Malibu and espresso or coffee liqueur. Following the frothing instructions given on page 38, froth the milk so that it has many tiny bubbles that barely form soft peaks. Top the espresso with the frothed milk.

1 SERVING

APPROXIMATE NUTRITIONAL ANALYSIS PER SERVING:

258 calories, 1g total fat, 1g saturated fat, 2mg cholesterol, 39mg sodium, 35g carbohydrates, 2g protein

Miss Felicita, it's your day! What are you doing right now? You're roasting coffee, and its wonderful flavour is wafting all around you?

—GUIDO GOZZANO

Espresso Eggnog

Eggnog, the traditional Christmas beverage of English ancestry, has been adapted and modified time and again. The following version contains espresso, which I believe adds a nice touch. Rather than just serve it for the holidays, why not prepare a batch and serve it instead of coffee the next time you have a group of friends over?

4 Caffè Lungo (16 ounces total, page 47)
3 large eggs
1 cup half-and-half
1 cup milk
1/4 cup granulated sugar
1/2 cup brandy
1 cup dark rum
Soft whipped cream (optional)
Grated nutmeg

Brew the caffè lungo and set aside. In a medium-size mixing bowl, beat the eggs until thick and lemon-colored. Blend in the half-and-half, milk, and sugar. Pour into the top of a double boiler over simmering water. Heat, stirring constantly, for 5 minutes, or until the mixture reaches 160°F on an instant-read thermometer (see note). Remove from the heat and pour through a fine-mesh strainer into a large mixing bowl. Blend in the brandy, rum, and espresso. Serve warm or let cool to room temperature. Serve in small cups or glasses with whipped cream, if desired. Sprinkle with nutmeg.

Note: The 160°F temperature is necessary for avoiding the risk of salmonella from the eggs.

10 SERVINGS

APPROXIMATE NUTRITIONAL ANALYSIS PER SERVING:

152 calories, 4g total fat, 2g saturated fat, 11mg cholesterol, 41mg sodium, 7g carbohydrates, 3g protein

San Francisco Cappuccino

This very adult version of hot chocolate will easily warm you up, even on the chilliest of days.

- 4 ounces (1/2 cup) frothed milk (page 38)
- 1 tablespoon good-quality chocolate syrup or sweetened cocoa powder
- 1 ounce brandy
- Granulated sugar (optional)

Following the frothing instructions given on page 38, froth the milk so that it has many tiny bubbles that barely form soft peaks. Pour the chocolate syrup and brandy into an Irish coffee glass (a special 6- to 8-ounce glass mug traditionally used to serve Irish coffee) and add the frothed milk. Sweeten with sugar, if desired. Stir to blend.

1 SERVING

APPROXIMATE NUTRITIONAL ANALYSIS PER SERVING:

156 calories, 2g total fat, 1g saturated fat, 5mg cholesterol, 80mg sodium, 17g carbohydrates, 4g protein

Caffè Borgia

For years people have been joining together the flavors and aroma of oranges, chocolate, and coffee in different confections and beverages. This is my version of an espresso drink served at a small, out-of-the-way café in New York's Greenwich Village.

- 1 thin slice orange, cut in half to fit in cup
- 1 Espresso (1½ ounces, page 45)
- 2 ounces (¼ cup) frothed milk (page 38)
- ½ teaspoon unsweetened cocoa powder
- 1 teaspoon granulated sugar
- Soft whipped cream
- Ground cinnamon

Gently squeeze the orange slice into a warmed large coffee cup or French coffee bowl. Brew the espresso into a warmed 2-ounce espresso or demitasse cup. Following the frothing instructions given on page 38, froth the milk so that it has many tiny bubbles that barely form soft peaks. Add the cocoa powder and sugar and stir to blend well. Pour into the prepared coffee cup simultaneously with the brewed espresso. Top with whipped cream and sprinkle with cinnamon.

1 SERVING

APPROXIMATE NUTRITIONAL ANALYSIS PER SERVING:

93 calories, 5g total fat, 3g saturated fat, 18mg cholesterol, 36mg sodium, 11g carbohydrates, 3g protein

South-of-the-Border Espresso

Tequila and orange-flavored Cointreau add a south-of-the-border flavor to this spirited espresso drink.

- 1 teaspoon firmly packed brown sugar
- 1 Caffè Lungo (3 ounces, page 47)
- 1 ounce tequila
- 1 ounce Cointreau

Place the sugar in a warmed 6-ounce cappuccino or coffee cup. Brew the caffè lungo into the cup. Pour in the tequila and Cointreau.

1 SERVING

APPROXIMATE NUTRITIONAL ANALYSIS PER SERVING:

198 calories, 0g total fat, 0g saturated fat, 0mg cholesterol, 7mg sodium, 19g carbohydrates, 0g protein

Divina Flor, who was just beginning to blossom out, served Santiago Nasar with a mug of country coffee, laced with sugar-cane alcohol, just as she always did every Monday, to help him get over the previous night's fatigue.

—GABRIEL GARCÍA MÁRQUEZ,
CHRONICLE OF A DEATH FORETOLD

Café Mexicano

Traditional Mexican coffee is called *café de olla*. It is usually brewed in an earthenware pot with cinnamon sticks and cloves and then sweetened with *piloncillo*—unrefined Mexican sugar. The following recipe is a close approximation.

- 1 teaspoon dark brown sugar, packed
- 1 Caffè Lungo (3 ounces, page 47)
- 3 ounces (heaping 1/3 cup) frothed milk (page 38)
- Ground cinnamon
- Ground cloves

Place the sugar in a warmed 6-ounce cappuccino or coffee cup. Brew the caffè lungo into the cup. Following the frothing instructions on page 38, froth the milk so that it has many tiny bubbles that barely form soft peaks. Pour in the frothed milk and sprinkle with cinnamon and cloves to taste.

1 SERVING

APPROXIMATE NUTRITIONAL ANALYSIS PER SERVING:

50 calories, 1g total fat, 1g saturated fat, 4mg cholesterol, 50mg sodium, 7g carbohydrates, 3g protein

Espresso Liqueur

You will be surprised at how easy it is to make delicious, homemade espresso liqueur. In fact, why not pour some into decorative bottles or decanters for those coffee aficionados on your holiday gift list?

2 cups Espresso Syrup (page 84)
1½ cups good-quality vodka
¼ cup espresso coffee beans

Mix together the syrup and vodka and pour, along with the espresso beans, into a clean glass bottle or jar with a tight-fitting stopper or lid. Store in a cool, dark place at least 1 week before serving. Consume within one month.

3½ CUPS

APPROXIMATE NUTRITIONAL ANALYSIS PER 1-OUNCE (2-TABLESPOON) SERVING:

108 calories, 0g total fat, 0g saturated fat, 0mg cholesterol, 1mg sodium, 17g carbohydrates, 0g protein

Espresso Flavorings and Cold Drinks

Besides being a beverage, coffee is a flavoring that bakers and cooks have been using for years. While it is not always possible to find coffee extract, it is extremely easy to reduce espresso to a strong, flavorful concentrate that can be added to other ingredients when preparing desserts and sweets such as the ones in Part Two of this book. Espresso Syrup, a sweet alternative to the concentrate, imparts a milder, sweet coffee flavor.

The recipes in this section consist of popular cold drinks and beverages made for the most part with Espresso Concentrate or Syrup. They are wonderful to enjoy al fresco on a hot summer afternoon or evening.

Espresso Concentrate

Homemade espresso concentrate enables you to add rich coffee flavor to an endless assortment of batters, custards, creams, and mousses. Since the flavor is so intense, always add a small amount at first so as not to overwhelm the other flavors. Since natural oils in coffee can burn and make the coffee taste bitter, you want to reduce the espresso as quickly as possible. The best way to do this is to bring the espresso to a rolling boil in a heavy-bottomed saucepan. After the espresso has reduced sufficiently, cool it down quickly by pouring it into a heatproof glass container placed in a large bowl of cold water.

5 Doppio Espresso (15 ounces total, page 48)

Prepare the espresso. Pour into a heavy-bottomed, medium-size saucepan and bring to a rolling boil. Monitor the pot so the espresso does not boil over. Let reduce to 3/4 cup. Pour the hot espresso concentrate into a heavy heatproof glass container such as a 2-cup Pyrex measure. Carefully place the container in an ice-water bath until the concentrate is cool. Store the cooled concentrate in a sealed jar or bottle in the refrigerator for up to three days. The concentrate can also be frozen for up to 3 months. Fill each compartment of an ice-cube tray with 1 tablespoon of the cooled espresso concentrate. When frozen, remove from tray and store in plastic bags.

3/4 CUP

APPROXIMATE NUTRITIONAL ANALYSIS PER TABLESPOON:

0 calories, 0g total fat, 0g saturated fat, 0mg cholesterol, 1mg sodium, 0g carbohydrates, 0g protein

Espresso Syrup

Espresso syrup, another handy flavoring to have in the kitchen, is also easy to prepare. This rich coffee syrup can be used as a sweet flavoring in many recipes or by itself, served warm on pancakes or waffles.

4 Caffè Ristretto (4 ounces total, page 46)
3/4 cup granulated sugar
1/4 cup water

Prepare the caffè ristretto. Set aside. In a small saucepan, combine the sugar and water and bring to a boil. Lower the heat and let simmer 5 minutes. Remove from the heat and let cool 1 minute. Stir in the brewed espresso. Let sit at least 30 minutes before using. Store in a sealed jar or bottle in the refrigerator up to 1 week.

APPROXIMATELY 1 CUP

APPROXIMATE NUTRITIONAL ANALYSIS PER TABLESPOON:

36 calories, 0g total fat, 0g saturated fat, 0mg cholesterol, 1mg sodium, 9g carbohydrates, 0g protein

You are the one, divine coffee, whose sweet liquor, without altering the mind, can make the heart bloom.

—ABBÉ DELILLE

Iced Espresso

This cool, refreshing pick-me-up is perfect for a hot, sultry day.

½ cup crushed ice
1 Doppio Espresso
(3 ounces, page 48)
Granulated sugar
Soft whipped cream or anisette
(optional)

Pack the crushed ice into an attractive but heatproof lowball glass. Prepare the espresso and pour, hot, over the ice. Sweeten with sugar to taste. Serve with a dollop of whipped cream or a shot of anisette, if desired.

1 SERVING

APPROXIMATE NUTRITIONAL ANALYSIS PER SERVING:

0 calories, 0g total fat, 0g saturated fat, 0mg cholesterol, 3mg sodium, 0g carbohydrates, 0g protein

Espresso Fizz

As mentioned on page 55, there exists a wide variety of flavored sweetened syrups from Italy for imparting additional flavor to espresso and frothed milk drinks. Prior to the days of Coke and Pepsi, it was very fashionable in Italian bars and cafés to order flavored fizzy beverages similar to the Espresso Fizz here.

3 tablespoons Espresso Syrup
(page 84)
Ice cubes
Cold seltzer or soda water

Pour the syrup into a tall 12-ounce glass. Fill with ice and soda water. Stir to blend.

1 SERVING

APPROXIMATE NUTRITIONAL ANALYSIS PER SERVING:

36 calories, 0g total fat, 0g saturated fat, 0mg cholesterol, 50mg sodium, 9g carbohydrates, 0g protein

Espresso Egg Cream

An egg cream is the most famous of New York soda fountain beverages. It does not contain a single egg, but derives its name from the foamy head that develops when the seltzer is mixed with the milk, a head that resembles frothy beaten egg white. Espresso Egg Cream makes for a delicious variation.

- 1 Caffè Ristretto (1 ounce, page 46)
- 1 teaspoon granulated sugar
- 1 cup cold milk
- Cold seltzer or soda water

Brew the caffè ristretto into a room-temperature 2-ounce espresso or demitasse cup. Let cool. Pour the espresso, sugar, and milk into a tall 12-ounce glass. Stir to blend. Fill with soda water while stirring with a spoon.

Mocha Egg Cream:

Eliminate the sugar and add 2 tablespoons chocolate syrup.

1 SERVING

APPROXIMATE NUTRITIONAL ANALYSIS PER SERVING OF ESPRESSO EGG CREAM:

118 calories, 3g total fat, 2g saturated fat, 10mg cholesterol, 149mg sodium, 16g carbohydrates, 8g protein

APPROXIMATE NUTRITIONAL ANALYSIS PER SERVING OF MOCHA EGG CREAM:

184 calories, 3g total fat, 2g saturated fat, 10mg cholesterol, 185mg sodium, 34g carbohydrates, 9g protein

PART TWO

ESPRESSO DESSERTS

Frozen Espresso Desserts

Espresso Cakes, Pastries, Custards, and Cookies

Espresso Sweets and Candies

Frozen Espresso Desserts

Ice cream and frozen desserts were first created in Italy in the time of the Roman Empire. Since the sixteenth century, Italians have been combining their love of frozen desserts with coffee. The smoothness and subtleties of well-brewed espresso reaches a new dimension when combined with cream and eggs in Italian ice cream, or gelato, and when mixed with sugar and frozen to semisolid to prepare a refreshing granita.

The recipes in this section pay homage to the frozen coffee desserts of Italy, as well as presenting American and European adaptations and creations.

Cappuccino Gelato

Gelato, or Italian ice cream, is usually much richer than traditional American ice cream. Made with light cream and egg yolks, Cappuccino Gelato is true to its origins.

4 cups light cream
1 cup espresso coffee beans, coarsely crushed
4 large egg yolks
1 cup granulated sugar

In a medium-size saucepan, bring the cream and coffee beans to a boil. Remove from the heat, cover, and let sit 15 minutes. Pour into a large Pyrex measure through a fine mesh strainer. Discard the coffee beans.

In a large mixing bowl, beat together the egg yolks and sugar until light and creamy. Pour the warm coffee-flavored cream into the egg yolk mixture, whisking continuously. Pour the custard mixture through the strainer into a clean medium-size saucepan. Cook over low heat, stirring continuously, until the mixture begins to thicken and coats the back of the spoon. Do not let boil or the custard may separate. Pour into a clean bowl, cover, and let cool to room temperature. Refrigerate when cool at least 4 hours or overnight, until the mixture is very cold.

Prepare an ice cream maker according to the manufacturer's instructions. Pour the cold custard mixture into the ice cream maker and proceed according to instructions. If you do not have an ice cream maker, pour the cold custard into a shallow, 6-to 8-cup plastic container. Cover with aluminum foil and freeze until set, stirring every 20 to 30 minutes with a fork to break up the ice crystals.

Store the frozen gelato in an airtight plastic container in the freezer. To reduce the chance of ice crystals developing, cover the surface of the gelato with a sheet of wax paper before covering with the lid.

8 SERVINGS (APPROXIMATELY 1 QUART)

APPROXIMATE NUTRITIONAL ANALYSIS PER SERVING:

475 calories, 40g total fat, 24g saturated fat, 239mg cholesterol, 45mg sodium, 29g carbohydrates, 4g protein

Mocha Fudge Sauce

This is the quintessential chocolate sauce for a decadent hot fudge sundae!

1 cup unsweetened cocoa powder
2/3 cup granulated sugar
1/2 cup light brown sugar, packed
1 cup light cream
4 Caffè Ristretto (4 ounces total, page 46)
1/2 cup unsalted butter, at room temperature, cut into small pieces
1 1/2 teaspoons vanilla extract

In a medium-size saucepan, whisk together the cocoa and sugars. Add the cream, espresso, and butter. Bring to a boil. Lower heat to medium and continue cooking, stirring constantly, for 1 minute. Remove from the heat and stir in the vanilla. Let cool to room temperature. Store in a covered jar in the refrigerator up to 1 week.

APPROXIMATELY 2 3/4 CUPS

APPROXIMATE NUTRITIONAL ANALYSIS PER 1/4-CUP SERVING:

229 calories, 16g total fat, 10g saturated fat, 47mg cholesterol, 13mg sodium, 24g carbohydrates, 2g protein

Mocha Buttered Almond Ice Cream

Mocha Buttered Almond Ice Cream is a wonderful combination of two of my favorite ice creams—coffee and chocolate—along with the buttery crunch of almond slivers.

- 1/2 tablespoon unsalted butter
- 1/3 cup slivered almonds
- 1/2 cup espresso coffee beans, coarsely crushed
- 4 cups light cream
- 2 large egg yolks
- 1 cup granulated sugar
- 1/4 cup unsweetened cocoa powder

Melt the butter in a small skillet over low heat. Add the almonds and brown until golden, stirring constantly. Remove the almonds to paper towels and pat to remove excess butter.

In a medium-size saucepan, bring the cream and coffee beans to a boil. Remove from the heat, cover, and let sit 15 minutes. Pour into a large Pyrex measure through a fine-mesh strainer. Discard the coffee beans.

In a large mixing bowl, beat together the egg yolks, sugar, and cocoa powder until crumbly. Pour the warm coffee-flavored cream into the egg yolk mixture, whisking continuously. Pour the custard mixture through the strainer into a clean medium-size saucepan. Cook over low heat, stirring continuously, until the mixture begins to thicken and coats the back of the spoon. Do not let boil or the custard may separate. Pour into a clean bowl, cover, and let cool to room temperature. Refrigerate when cool at least 4 hours or overnight, until the mixture is very cold. Stir in the toasted almonds.

Prepare an ice cream maker according to the manufacturer's instructions. Pour the cold custard into the ice cream maker and proceed according to instructions. If you do not have an ice cream maker, pour the cold custard into a shallow, 6- to 8-cup plastic container. Cover with aluminum foil and freeze until set, stirring every 20 to 30 minutes with a fork to break up the ice crystals.

Store the frozen ice cream in an airtight plastic container in the freezer. To reduce the chance of ice crystals developing, cover the surface of the ice cream with a sheet of wax paper before covering with the lid.

8 SERVINGS (APPROXIMATELY 1 QUART)

APPROXIMATE NUTRITIONAL ANALYSIS PER SERVING:

506 calories, 42g total fat, 24g saturated fat, 187mg cholesterol, 44mg sodium, 31g carbohydrates, 5g protein

Mocha Ice Cream Cake

I have never seen anyone turn down a slice of ice cream cake, especially when it is homemade!

- 1 recipe sponge cake batter from recipe for Italian Celebration Cake (page 107)
- 1 recipe Mocha Buttered Almond Ice Cream (page 95) or 1 quart any good-quality coffee-flavored ice cream, softened
- 1 cup heavy cream
- 3 tablespoons granulated sugar
- 1/3 cup sliced almonds
- 2 ounces semisweet chocolate, grated

Bake the sponge cake in a 9-inch springform pan. When the cake has cooled, slice in three equal layers. Place one layer, cut side up, in the bottom of the same pan that was used for baking the cake. Spread half of the ice cream over the cake layer. Cover with another cake layer and spread this with the remaining ice cream. Cover with the last cake layer, right side up. Press down gently. Cover with a double layer of foil and freeze overnight.

Whip the heavy cream until soft peaks form. Gradually add the sugar and continue whipping until very thick.

Remove the ice cream cake from the freezer. Slide a sharp knife around the edge of the cake to loosen it from the sides of the pan. Frost the top and sides of the cake evenly with the whipped cream. Gently press the sliced almonds into the sides of the cake and sprinkle the top with the grated chocolate. Return to the freezer until the whipped cream is frozen.

10 SERVINGS

APPROXIMATE NUTRITIONAL ANALYSIS PER SERVING:

679 calories, 48g total fat, 27g saturated fat, 246mg cholesterol, 377mg sodium, 58g carbohydrates, 10g protein

Frozen Cappuccino

This frozen cappuccino mousse should be prepared early in the day or the day before you plan to serve it. Rich in coffee flavor, it makes for a delicious, light dessert.

- 1/2 cup espresso coffee beans, coarsely crushed
- 2 cups light cream
- 2 large eggs, separated, plus 2 large egg whites
- 3/4 cup granulated sugar
- 2 tablespoons unsweetened cocoa powder

In a medium-size saucepan bring the cream and coffee beans to a boil. Remove from heat, cover, and let sit 15 minutes. Pour into a 2- to 4-cup Pyrex measure through a fine-mesh strainer. Discard the coffee beans.

In a large mixing bowl, beat together the egg yolks and 1/2 cup of the sugar until light and creamy. Pour the warm coffee-flavored cream into the egg yolk mixture, whisking continuously. Pour the custard mixture through the strainer into a clean medium-size saucepan. Cook over low heat, stirring continuously, until the mixture begins to thicken and coats the back of the spoon. Do not let boil or the custard may separate. Pour into a clean bowl, cover, and let cool to room temperature. Refrigerate when cool at least 4 hours or overnight, until the mixture is very cold.

Chill a 6-cup soufflé dish or serving bowl at least 1 hour in the freezer. In a large mixing bowl, beat the 4 egg whites until soft peaks form. Gradually add the sugar and beat until stiff. Fold the chilled custard mixture into the stiff egg whites. Pour into the chilled dish. Cover with a double layer of aluminum foil and freeze overnight.

Before serving, sprinkle the cocoa powder, through a fine sieve or tea strainer, over the top.

8 SERVINGS

APPROXIMATE NUTRITIONAL ANALYSIS PER SERVING:

269 calories, 20g total fat, 12g saturated fat, 119mg cholesterol, 37mg sodium, 21g carbohydrates, 3g protein

Vanilla Cappuccino

The components of traditional cappuccino are used in this frozen dessert version that is quick and easy to prepare.

2 Caffè Ristretto (1 ounce each, page 46)
$^{1}/_{4}$ cup heavy cream, whipped to soft peaks
2 large scoops good-quality vanilla ice cream
2 tablespoons Espresso Syrup (page 84)

Divide the brewed espresso between two dessert bowls. Top each with half of the whipped cream and a scoop of ice cream. Drizzle with the espresso syrup.

2 SERVINGS

APPROXIMATE NUTRITIONAL ANALYSIS PER SERVING:

281 calories, 19g total fat, 12g saturated fat, 68mg cholesterol, 64mg sodium, 26g carbohydrates, 3g protein

Coffee Parfaits

Ice cream parfaits add a nice touch to a special meal. Simple to prepare, these coffee parfaits will be especially welcome on a hot summer's night.

- 1 pint good-quality vanilla ice cream, slightly softened
- 1/2 cup Espresso Syrup (page 84)
- 1/2 cup heavy cream, whipped and sweetened with 1 tablespoon granulated sugar
- 4 Chocolate-Covered Espresso Beans (optional; page 145)

In four parfait glasses or goblets, layer the ice cream, syrup, and whipped cream (2 layers each), ending with a final layer of cream. Top each parfait with a chocolate-covered espresso bean, if desired.

4 SERVINGS

APPROXIMATE NUTRITIONAL ANALYSIS PER SERVING:

(without chocolate-covered espresso beans)

269 calories, 13g total fat, 8g saturated fat, 49mg cholesterol, 60mg sodium, 38g carbohydrates, 3g protein

WHITE AND BLACK

A *blanco y negro,* or a "white and black," is a popular Spanish alternative to the traditional afternoon cup of café con leche. You will be amazed how delicious something as simple as a scoop of vanilla ice cream in a cup of espresso can be.

1 scoop good-quality vanilla ice cream
1 Doppio Espresso (3 ounces, page 48)

Place the ice cream in a large coffee cup or a lowball glass. Pour the brewed espresso over the ice cream.

1 SERVING

APPROXIMATE NUTRITIONAL ANALYSIS PER SERVING:

67 calories, 4g total fat, 3g saturated fat, 15mg cholesterol, 30mg sodium, 8g carbohydrates, 1g protein

Drink plenty of it: in its flavour worries disappear—and its fire burns away the dark thoughts of everyday life.

—HADJIBUN (ARABIAN JURIST)

Espresso Milk Shake

An American original with an Italian touch.

- 2 scoops Cappuccino Gelato (page 93) or good-quality coffee ice cream
- 1 cup milk
- 2 tablespoons Espresso Syrup (page 84)

Place the ice cream, milk, and syrup in a blender jar. Blend until smooth. Pour into a large, tall glass.

1 SERVING

APPROXIMATE NUTRITIONAL ANALYSIS PER SERVING:

350 calories, 12g total fat, 8g saturated fat, 48mg cholesterol, 194mg sodium, 51g carbohydrates, 11g protein

> *Among the numerous luxuries of the table, unknown to our forefathers, coffee may be considered as one of the most valuable. Its taste is very agreeable, and its flavour uncommonly so; but its principal excellence depends on its salubrity, and on its exhilarating quality. It excites cheerfulness, without intoxication; and the pleasing flow of spirits which it occasions . . . is never followed by sadness, languor or debility. It defuses over the whole frame a glow of health, and sense of ease and well-being which is extremely delightful: existence is felt to be a positive enjoyment, and the mental powers are awakened and rendered uncommonly active.*
>
> —BENJAMIN THOMPSON

Espresso Granita

Granita, the classic Italian frozen dessert, is enjoyed in cafés throughout Italy during the summer. Not as firm as sorbet, granita should be soft enough to eat with a spoon and straw.

- 4 Doppio Espresso (16 ounces total, page 48), at room temperature
- 1 cup Espresso Syrup (page 84), chilled
- 2 tablespoons anisette or 1 teaspoon grated lemon zest (optional)
- Soft whipped cream (optional)

In a medium-size mixing bowl, stir together the espresso and syrup. Add the optional anisette or lemon zest, if desired. Cover and refrigerate at least 4 hours or overnight, until the mixture is very cold.

Prepare an ice cream maker according to the manufacturer's instructions. Pour the granita mixture into the ice cream maker and proceed according to instructions. Do not let the granita freeze solid. It will be ready when it turns into a medium-firm slush. If you do not have an ice cream maker, pour the cold mixture into a shallow 4-cup plastic container. Cover with aluminum foil and freeze until set, stirring every 20 to 30 minutes with a fork to break up the ice crystals. Granita is ready to serve when the mixture is a medium-firm slush.

Serve the granita in glasses with anisette, lemon zest, or soft, unsweetened whipped cream, if desired. Eat with a spoon and straw.

4 SERVINGS

APPROXIMATE NUTRITIONAL ANALYSIS PER SERVING:

173 calories, 0g total fat, 0g saturated fat, 0mg cholesterol, 6mg sodium, 41g carbohydrates, 0g protein

Mocha Frappé

Falling somewhere between an egg cream and a shake, a mocha frappé is a surefire way to cool off on the hottest of summer days.

- 1 cup finely crushed or shaved ice
- 2 Caffè Lungo (6 ounces total, page 47), cooled to room temperature
- 2 tablespoons granulated sugar
- 3 tablespoons chocolate syrup
- Whipped cream

Place the crushed ice, espresso, sugar, and chocolate syrup in a blender. Blend until the frappé is smooth and frothy. Pour into tall glasses. Serve with a dollop of whipped cream and a straw.

2 SERVINGS

APPROXIMATE NUTRITIONAL ANALYSIS PER SERVING:

136 calories, 3g total fat, 2g saturated fat, 10mg cholesterol, 33mg sodium, 29g carbohydrates, 1g protein

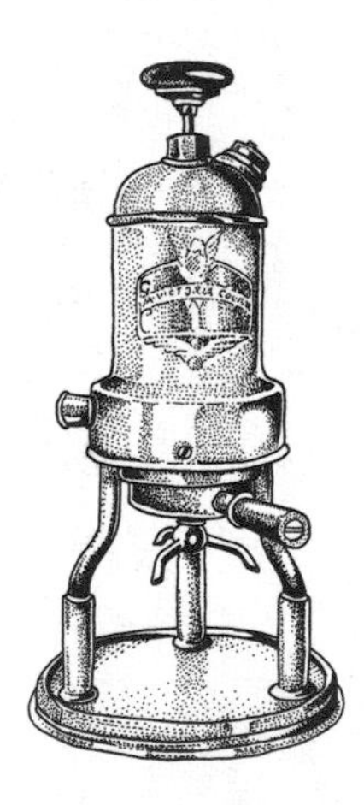

Espresso Cakes, Pastries, Custards, and Cookies

While researching this book, I was pleasantly surprised by the number of traditional dessert recipes I encountered that had strong coffee in them as a primary ingredient. Many of these recipes are now relatively forgotten; I can only assume that this is attributable to the popularity of that other caffeine-rich ingredient, chocolate.

By using these classic recipes as a source of inspiration, I began to modify and adapt other confections by adding espresso and espresso flavorings, the results of which I found to be wonderfully delicious. I hope that you enjoy the following desserts as much as my family, friends, and I have.

ITALIAN CELEBRATION CAKE

Over the years, this has become the most requested cake in our home for birthdays and other celebrations. Besides looking beautiful, it is extremely easy to prepare and assemble.

Espresso Pastry Cream

- 2½ cups milk
- ½ cup espresso coffee beans, coarsely crushed
- 4 large eggs plus four large egg yolks
- 1 cup granulated sugar
- 4 tablespoons unbleached all-purpose flour

Sponge Cake

- 1 cup unbleached all-purpose flour
- 1 teaspoon baking powder
- 4 large eggs, separated, plus 1 whole large egg
- ⅔ cup granulated sugar
- Pinch of salt

To Assemble

- 2 tablespoons dark rum mixed with ¼ cup water (optional)
- 1 package (3 ounces) soft ladyfingers
- ⅓ cup sliced almonds

Prepare the pastry cream: In a medium-size saucepan, bring the milk and coffee beans to a boil. Remove from the heat, cover, and let sit 10 minutes. Pour into a second saucepan through a fine-mesh strainer. Discard the coffee beans

In a large mixing bowl, beat together the whole eggs, yolks, sugar, and flour until well combined. Bring the coffee-flavored milk to a boil. Lower the heat and gradually whisk in the egg mixture. Stir constantly until the pastry cream begins to thicken and comes to a boil. Remove from the heat and pour the cream into a nonreactive bowl. Cover with a piece of plastic wrap, pushing the plastic into the custard so that a skin does not form. Let cool to room temperature.

Prepare the sponge cake: Preheat the oven to 375°F. Butter and flour a 9-inch round cake pan.

Sift the flour and baking powder into a mixing bowl. Set aside. Beat the egg yolks, whole egg, and 1/3 cup of the sugar in a large mixing bowl until the mixture is thick and lemon-colored. Fold in the flour mixture. Set the batter aside. In a large bowl, beat the egg whites with a pinch of salt until stiff peaks form. Gradually add the remaining 1/3 cup sugar and beat until glossy. Fold one-third of the batter into the beaten egg whites, until just incorporated. Repeat the process two more times.

Pour the batter into the prepared pan and bake until the cake is golden and springs back when lightly pressed, 20 to 25 minutes. Let cool 10 minutes, then remove the cake to a wire rack to cool completely.

Assemble the dessert: When the cake has cooled, slice it in half horizontally. Place one half, cut side up, on a large serving plate. Sprinkle, if desired, with half of the diluted rum, then spread with one-third of the pastry cream. Place the second layer of cake, right side up, on top of the pastry cream. Sprinkle, if desired, with the remaining diluted rum, then spread with half of the remaining pastry cream. Break the ladyfingers in half. Attach them around the perimeter of the cake, broken side down, by spreading them with the remaining pastry cream. Cover the top with the sliced almonds.

Variation:

To make this cake with vanilla pastry cream, eliminate steeping the coffee beans in the milk. Instead, heat the milk with the grated zest of 1 lemon, and add 2 teaspoons vanilla extract to the pastry cream after transferring it to the nonreactive bowl.

8 SERVINGS

APPROXIMATE NUTRITIONAL ANALYSIS PER SERVING:

388 calories, 9g total fat, 2g saturated fat, 252mg cholesterol, 94mg sodium, 65g carbohydrates, 11g protein

Cappuccino Pudding Cake

Although relatively unknown today, pudding cakes were quite popular during the days of our founding fathers. The liquid batter separates during the baking to form a rich, flanlike top layer and a light sponge-cake bottom.

- 2 tablespoons unsalted butter, at room temperature
- 2/3 cup granulated sugar
- 1/8 teaspoon salt
- 3 large eggs, separated, plus one large egg white
- 1/4 cup unbleached all-purpose flour
- 1 cup milk
- 4 Caffè Ristretto (4 ounces total, page 46), cooled to room temperature

Preheat the oven to 325°F. Lightly butter a 9-inch round cake pan.

Place the butter in a large mixing bowl and cut in the sugar and salt until crumbly. Add the egg yolks and whisk together until well blended. Add the flour and mix with the whisk until smooth. Slowly whisk in the milk and cooled espresso. Set aside.

In a large mixing bowl, beat the egg whites with a pinch of salt to stiff, moist peaks. Gently fold into the batter and spread in the prepared pan. Set the pan into a larger pan and place in the oven. Fill the larger pan with boiling water so that it comes halfway up the sides of the cake pan. Bake approximately 25 minutes, or until the cake is set and does not wobble when shaken.

Remove from the oven. Let the cake cool 10 minutes in the water bath. Remove the pan from the water bath, run a sharp knife around the edge of the cake, and invert onto a lightly buttered cake pan. Can be served warm.

8 SERVINGS

APPROXIMATE NUTRITIONAL ANALYSIS PER SERVING:

148 calories, 5g total fat, 3g saturated fat, 89mg cholesterol, 80mg sodium, 21g carbohydrates, 4g protein

FALLEN MOCHA SOUFFLÉ

This is one of those recipes that you save to make for a very special occasion. Although it is very easy to prepare, it is extremely rich and worth every single calorie! The batter does not bake evenly, forming a brownielike crust with a fudge and chocolate mousse–like center. Without a doubt, this cake is a chocoholic's dream come true!

16 ounces good-quality semisweet chocolate, chopped or morsels
1 cup (2 sticks) unsalted butter, cut into pieces
1/4 cup Espresso Syrup (page 84)
9 large eggs, separated
1 1/4 cups granulated sugar
Pinch of salt

Preheat the oven to 350°F. Butter and flour a 10-inch springform pan.

Melt the chocolate and butter in the top of a double boiler over simmering water. Stir until smooth. Remove from the heat and let cool to room temperature. Stir in the espresso syrup.

In a large mixing bowl, beat the egg yolks and the sugar with an electric mixer for approximately 5 to 10 minutes, or until thick and pale in color. In another large bowl, beat the egg whites with a pinch of salt until they just begin to hold stiff peaks. Fold one-third of the chocolate mixture into the egg yolk mixture, then fold in one-third of the egg whites. Repeat the process twice more with the remaining chocolate mixture and egg whites. Spoon the mixture into the prepared pan and bake for 25 to 30 minutes, or until the edges have puffed up (the center will not be set). Remove from the oven and let the soufflé cool to room temperature on a wire rack. Cover and chill overnight.

When ready to serve, run a sharp knife around the outside of the soufflé to loosen it from the sides of the pan. Carefully remove the pan sides. Cut the soufflé into thin slices with a knife dipped in hot water.

16 SERVINGS

APPROXIMATE NUTRITIONAL ANALYSIS PER SERVING:

348 calories, 23g total fat, 13g saturated fat, 150mg cholesterol, 156mg sodium, 36g carbohydrates, 5g protein

Mocha Cocoa Cake

This is one of my favorite chocolate cake recipes. It is easy to prepare, has a rich chocolate taste, and best of all is very low in cholesterol. It is so moist that it will stay fresh for close to a week, improving in flavor every day.

1¾ cups unbleached all-purpose flour
¾ cup unsweetened cocoa powder
1 teaspoon baking soda
¼ teaspoon salt
1 cup granulated sugar
¾ cup nonfat plain yogurt
5 Espresso (7½ ounces total, page 45)
½ cup vegetable oil

Preheat the oven to 350°F. Butter and flour a 9-inch Bundt pan.

Sift together the flour, cocoa powder, baking soda, and salt into a large mixing bowl. In another large bowl, mix together the sugar, yogurt, espresso, and oil until well blended. Pour the liquid ingredients into the flour mixture and mix together just until blended. Spoon the batter into the prepared pan, smooth with a spatula, and bake 30 minutes, or until a tester comes out clean. Remove from the oven and let cool 10 minutes before removing from the pan.

8 SERVINGS

APPROXIMATE NUTRITIONAL ANALYSIS PER SERVING:

349 calories, 15g total fat, 2g saturated fat, 1mg cholesterol, 88mg sodium, 52g carbohydrates, 6g protein

Butterscotch Espresso Pound Cake

The following blue-ribbon pound cake took first prize a few years ago at a local fair. So rich and moist, you will easily understand the judges' decision.

- 4 Caffè Ristretto (4 ounces total, page 46)
- 1 cup (6 ounces) butterscotch morsels
- 1 cup (2 sticks) unsalted butter, at room temperature
- 1½ cups granulated sugar
- 3 cups unbleached all-purpose flour
- ½ teaspoon baking soda
- ¼ teaspoon salt
- ¾ cup buttermilk
- 4 large eggs

Preheat the oven to 350°F.

In a medium-size saucepan over low heat, melt the butterscotch morsels in the espresso, stirring until smooth. Do not let boil. Remove from the heat and cool until lukewarm.

In a large mixing bowl, cream the butter and sugar until light and fluffy, using an electric mixer. Add the butterscotch mixture and beat with the mixer until thoroughly blended.

Sift together the flour, baking soda, and salt into a medium-size mixing bowl. Fold the flour mixture into the butterscotch mixture, alternating with the buttermilk. Mix at first on low and then beat on medium for 2 minutes. Add the eggs, one at a time, beating for 1 minute after each addition.

Pour the batter into the prepared pan and bake 55 to 60 minutes, or until a tester comes out clean. Cool in the pan 10 minutes. Remove from the pan to a wire rack to cool completely.

10 SERVINGS

APPROXIMATE NUTRITIONAL ANALYSIS PER SERVING:

518 calories, 24g total fat, 16g saturated fat, 51mg cholesterol, 341mg sodium, 71g carbohydrates, 7g protein

A cup of coffee detracts nothing from your intellect; on the contrary your stomach is freed by it and no longer distresses your brain; it will not hamper your mind with troubles but give freedom to its working. Suave molecules of Mocha stir up your blood without causing excessive heat; the organ of thought receives from it a feeling of sympathy; work becomes easier and you will sit down without distress to your principal repast which will restore your body and afford you a calm delicious night.

—CHARLES MAURICE DE TALLEYRAND-PÉRIGORD

Espresso Pecan Blondies

Blondies are like chewy brownies that don't have chocolate. These Espresso Pecan Blondies remind me of the wonderful pecan praline made in New Orleans.

- 1/2 cup unbleached all-purpose flour
- 1/2 teaspoon salt
- 1 teaspoon baking powder
- 1/4 cup (1/2 stick) unsalted butter
- 1 cup firmly packed light brown sugar
- 3 tablespoons Espresso Syrup (page 84)
- 1 large egg, lightly beaten
- 1/2 cup chopped pecans

Preheat the oven to 350°F. Grease an 8-inch square baking pan.

In a medium-size mixing bowl, stir together the flour, salt, and baking powder. Set aside. In a medium saucepan over medium heat, melt the butter and brown sugar, stirring to mix. Stir in the syrup and remove from the heat. Let cool 5 minutes. Stir in the egg and then the flour mixture. Add the pecans.

Spoon the batter into the prepared pan and smooth with a spatula. Bake 25 to 30 minutes, or until a tester comes out clean. Cool in the pan on a wire rack. Cut while still warm.

16 SERVINGS

APPROXIMATE NUTRITIONAL ANALYSIS PER SERVING:

107 calories, 5g total fat, 2g saturated fat, 8mg cholesterol, 37mg sodium, 14g carbohydrates, 1g protein

Mocha Cheesecake

This Mocha Cheesecake has a chocolate cookie crust that adds to its rich flavor. Since the cake has to continue baking in the cooling oven and then be refrigerated overnight, make it the day before you plan to serve it.

2 cups chocolate cookie crumbs (use plain chocolate wafers or chocolate graham crackers ground up in a food processor)
½ cup (1 stick) unsalted butter, melted
2½ packages (8 ounces each) cream cheese, at room temperature
1 cup granulated sugar
2 large eggs
½ cup plus 2 tablespoons heavy cream
¼ cup Espresso Concentrate (page 83)

Preheat the oven to 325°F.

In a medium-size mixing bowl, blend together the cookie crumbs and the melted butter. Line of the bottom of a 9-or 10-inch springform pan with a piece of baking parchment or wax paper cut to fit. Add the crumb mixture and spread evenly to cover the bottom of the pan, pressing down lightly with your fingertips.

In a large mixing bowl, cream the cream cheese with the sugar, using an electric mixer. Gradually beat in the eggs. Add the cream and espresso concentrate and continue beating until the mixture is smooth and creamy. Pour the cream cheese mixture into the prepared pan and bake for 30 minutes, or until the filling is set. Turn off the oven. Leave the cake in the oven to continue baking. Remove when the oven has cooled, approximately 4 hours later. Let cool to room temperature and chill overnight in the refrigerator before serving.

16 SERVINGS

APPROXIMATE NUTRITIONAL ANALYSIS PER SERVING:

309 calories, 21g total fat, 11g saturated fat, 53mg cholesterol, 233mg sodium, 27g carbohydrates, 4g protein

Swiss Chocolate Log

We first enjoyed this version of an icebox cake when we visited friends in Switzerland. When sliced thin, the cookies and chocolate form an attractive striped pattern.

- 12 ounces milk chocolate, chopped or morsels
- ½ cup (1 stick) unsalted butter
- 6 tablespoons Espresso Concentrate (page 83)
- 4 large eggs
- 1 box Social Tea cookies or similar-type biscuits

Cut strips of wax paper or baking parchment to line the sides, ends, and bottom of a greased 8-by 4-inch loaf pan. Butter the paper.

Preheat the oven to 300°F. Put the chocolate and butter in the top of a double boiler over simmering water. Cover until melted. Beat with a whisk to blend. In a small bowl, beat the eggs with a whisk, then whisk in the espresso concentrate. Slowly pour the espresso mixture into the chocolate mixture. Blend, still over simmering water, with the whisk, for 3 minutes. Remove from the heat.

Pour one-fourth of the chocolate mixture into the prepared loaf pan. First dipping the cookies into the remaining warm mixture to coat, place them horizontally in three rows down the length of the pan. Fill any wide gaps between the three rows with cookie pieces. Pour the remaining chocolate mixture over the prepared cookies to cover. Place in the oven for 15 minutes so that the warm chocolate softens the cookies. Cover with foil and let cool to room temperature. Refrigerate overnight.

Before serving, run a sharp knife around the inside perimeter of the pan. Turn the pan over and carefully remove the dessert. Peel off the paper and cut into thin slices, cutting straight down with a very sharp chef's knife.

16 SERVINGS

APPROXIMATE NUTRITIONAL ANALYSIS PER SERVING:

253 calories, 16g total fat, 8g saturated fat, 72mg cholesterol, 149mg sodium, 27g carbohydrates, 4g protein

Cappuccino Chiffon Pie

Chiffon pies were very popular in the sixties. The light, airy chiffon filling here is flavored with espresso and tastes like a creamy cappuccino.

- 1½ cups chocolate cookie crumbs (use plain chocolate wafers or chocolate graham crackers ground up in a food processor)
- 6 tablespoons (¾ stick) unsalted butter, melted
- ¼ cup water
- 1 tablespoon unflavored gelatin
- 3 large eggs, separated
- ¾ cup granulated sugar
- 3 tablespoon Espresso Concentrate (page 83)
- ¼ cup heavy cream

Preheat the oven to 325°F.

In a medium-size mixing bowl, blend together the cookie crumbs and the melted butter. Spread the crumbs evenly over the bottom and sides of a buttered 9-inch deep-dish pie plate, pressing down lightly with your fingertips. Bake 10 minutes. Remove from the oven and let cool a few minutes, then press up the crumbs if the sides have fallen slightly. Let cool to room temperature.

Heat the water in a small saucepan just until it begins to boil. Remove from the heat and sprinkle with the gelatin. Let stand 1 minute. Stir over low heat until the gelatin is completely dissolved. Do not boil.

In a medium-size bowl, beat the egg yolks with an electric mixer until thick and pale in color. Gradually add the sugar and continue beating until thick and light in color. Gradually add the espresso concentrate, heavy cream, and gelatin mixture. Mix until blended. In a large mixing bowl, using clean beaters, beat the egg whites to soft peaks. Gently fold the egg whites into the espresso mixture. Pour into the prepared pie shell and refrigerate at least 2 hours or overnight.

Note: Because this recipe contains raw eggs, avoid serving it to anyone to whom the risk of salmonella may cause health-related complications.

8 SERVINGS

APPROXIMATE NUTRITIONAL ANALYSIS PER SERVING:

330 calories, 15g total fat, 4g saturated fat, 90mg cholesterol, 260mg sodium, 46g carbohydrates, 5g protein

New Orleans Café au Lait Pecan Pie

Now you can enjoy your pie and coffee together in one dessert. One of my favorite pies, this variation of pecan pie is rich in flavor and not as sweet as the traditional version.

3 large eggs
2/3 cup light corn syrup
1/3 cup Espresso Syrup (page 84)
1 cup granulated sugar
3 tablespoons heavy cream
1 1/2 cups pecans
2 unbaked shallow 9-inch pie crusts

Preheat the oven to 350°F.

In a large mixing bowl, beat the eggs, then beat in the corn syrup, espresso syrup, sugar, and cream. Stir in the pecans. Pour into the pie crusts and bake 50 minutes, or until the centers have set. Cool on wire racks to room temperature.

16 SERVINGS

APPROXIMATE NUTRITIONAL ANALYSIS PER SERVING:

316 calories, 17g total fat, 4g saturated fat, 44mg cholesterol, 152mg sodium, 39g carbohydrates, 4g protein

Mocha Cannoli

The best known of all Italian pastries, homemade cannoli are much simpler to make than you can imagine. You can prepare the shells and the filling ahead of time, but be sure to assemble the cannoli right before serving so the shell doesn't get soggy. The cannoli dough is wrapped around stainless-steel cannoli tubes, which are available at most housewares stores and through catalogs.

Cannoli Shells

4 teaspoons sugar
4 teaspoons vegetable shortening
1 large egg, beaten
2 tablespoons white wine vinegar
2½ tablespoons water
2 teaspoons honey
1 teaspoon ground cinnamon
1½ cups unbleached all-purpose flour, or more as needed

Mocha Cannoli Cream

2 cups whole-milk ricotta
¼ cup granulated sugar
2 tablespoons Espresso Concentrate (page 83; see note)
3 tablespoons mini semisweet chocolate chips

To Finish the Dessert

Vegetable oil for frying
Confectioners' sugar for sprinkling

Prepare the cannoli dough: In a large mixing bowl, cream together the sugar and shortening, using an electric mixer. Mix in half of the beaten egg (approximately 2 tablespoons, reserving the remainder), vinegar, water, honey, and cinnamon. Gradually add the flour and mix until a stiff dough is formed. Add more flour if necessary. Form the dough into a flat circle. Wrap in plastic wrap and chill in the refrigerator at least 2 hours or overnight.

Prepare the cannoli cream: Place the ricotta in a large strainer lined with cheesecloth or a sheet of paper towel. Place over a large bowl, cover, and refrigerate overnight to drain.

In a large mixing bowl, combine the drained ricotta, sugar, and espresso concentrate. Beat on high with an electric mixer until smooth and creamy. Fold in the chocolate chips. Cover and chill in the refrigerator at least 2 hours or overnight.

Prepare the cannoli shells: When the dough has chilled sufficiently, gently roll it out on a lightly floured work surface until it is slightly less than 1/8 inch thick. You can also roll the dough out using a hand-cranked pasta maker as follows: Cut the dough into 4 equal pieces and shape into balls. Flatten each ball with the palm of your hand and sprinkle lightly with flour. Roll the dough through the pasta maker on the highest setting. Reinsert the dough and roll through the next succeedingly lower settings until the dough is 1/8 inch thick. Once the dough is rolled out, cut out as many 4-inch circles as possible. You should wind up with approximately 18 to 20 circles.

Lightly grease the cannoli tubes with vegetable oil or shortening. With the rolling pin, gently flatten each 4-inch circle of dough, in one direction only, so that it becomes oval (the oval should be slightly shorter than the cannoli tube). Wrap the dough oval around the cannoli tube. Lightly brush one edge with the reserved beaten egg to seal. Do not get egg on the tube or it will stick to the pastry. Continue until all the tubes are wrapped with dough.

Fry the cannoli shells: Heat 1 inch of vegetable oil in a medium-size, deep skillet to approximately 350°F. Fry the cannoli, two at a time, until lightly golden, about 6 to 8 minutes. Remove from the oil and drain on paper towels. While still warm, gently slide out the cannoli tube and repeat the process until all the shells are fried and the remaining dough has been used.

Fill the cannoli shells: When the shells are cooled and you are ready to serve, remove the filling from the refrigerator. Fill the shells by using either a teaspoon or a pastry bag fitted with a 3/4-inch plain, round tip. Dust with confectioners' sugar. Cannoli shells can be prepared and stored in an airtight container for up to 1 week before filling. If you like to plan very far in advance, you can store the unfilled shells in the freezer for up to 30 days.

Note: For traditional Sicilian cannoli, substitute 1 teaspoon vanilla extract for the espresso concentrate.

APPROXIMATELY 18 CANNOLI

APPROXIMATE NUTRITIONAL ANALYSIS PER CANNOLI:

149 calories, 8g total fat, 3g saturated fat, 27mg cholesterol, 27mg sodium, 16g carbohydrates, 6g protein

Petits Suisses

These miniature éclairs are a wonderful accompaniment to a cup of espresso or cappuccino. Simple to prepare, you can make the shells ahead of time and freeze them in an airtight container to be used at another time or when unannounced company drops in.

Pâte à Choux

1 cup water
½ cup (1 stick) unsalted butter, cut into small pieces
¼ teaspoon salt
1 cup unbleached all-purpose flour
4 large eggs, lightly beaten

Filling

1 recipe espresso pastry cream, from recipe for Italian Celebration Cake (page 107)

Glaze

1 cup confectioners' sugar
2 tablespoons plus 1 teaspoon Espresso Concentrate (page 83)

Bring the water to a boil in a medium-size saucepan. Add the butter and salt and lower to a simmer once the butter has melted. Add the flour all at once and beat with a wooden spoon until the mixture leaves the sides of the pan and forms a ball. Remove from the heat and transfer the dough to a large mixing bowl. Make a well in the center of the dough and add one-fourth of the beaten egg. Beat with a wooden spoon to combine. At first the dough will look slightly separated, which is normal. Add the remaining egg, one-third at a time, beating well after each addition. The dough is ready to use when it holds its shape when a small amount is lifted with a spoon.

Preheat the oven to 425°F. Line two baking sheets with baking parchment or butter lightly.

Fit a pastry bag with a 3/4-inch plain round tip. Fill the bag with the choux paste and pipe out 2-inch-long cylinders, 1 inch apart on the prepared baking sheets. (Alternatively, shape éclairs into 2-inch-long and 1/2-inch-wide cylinders using two teaspoons dipped in water.) Bake for 15 minutes. Pierce the baked éclairs with a fork and return to the oven an additional 5 minutes. Remove from the baking sheets and cool on wire racks.

Spoon the espresso pastry cream into a pastry bag fitted with a 1/8-inch plain round tip. Stick the tip into an end of the eclair and fill with a small amount of cream. (You can also fill the cooled eclairs with a teaspoon by slicing off a thin layer from the top of each. Fill with slightly less than 1/2 teaspoon of the espresso pastry cream, then replace the top.)

Prepare a glaze by mixing together the confectioners' sugar and espresso concentrate until smooth. Spread a thin layer of glaze over the filled éclairs.

APPROXIMATELY 60 PETITS SUISSES

APPROXIMATE NUTRITIONAL ANALYSIS PER PETIT SUISSE

61 calories, 3g total fat, 1g saturated fat, 47mg cholesterol, 39mg sodium, 8g carbohydrates, 2g protein

Espresso Squares

These buttercream-iced sponge cake squares are attractively adorned with an espresso bean. Serve with a bowl of fresh berries or sliced fruit for a wonderful end to a special meal.

- 1 recipe sponge cake batter from recipe for Italian Celebration Cake (page 107)
- 1 recipe Mocha Crème (opposite page)
- 16 espresso beans

Preheat the oven to 375°F. Line a 15- by 10-inch baking pan with a sheet of baking parchment. Butter and flour the paper.

Prepare the sponge cake batter as instructed. Spoon the batter into the pan and smooth evenly with a damp spatula. Bake approximately 10 to 15 minutes, or until lightly golden and the cake springs back when lightly pressed. Cool in the pan on a wire rack.

Prepare the mocha crème. When the cake has cooled, invert it onto a clean kitchen towel. Peel off the baking parchment. Trim the edges with a sharp knife and cut crosswise in half so that you have two 10- by 7½-inch layers. Spread half of the mocha crème on one layer. Cover with the remaining layer. Frost the top of the cake with the remaining crème. Using the tines of a fork or an icing comb, trace a pattern of lines in the frosting. With a sharp knife, cut the cake into 4 lengthwise strips. Cut each strip into 4 equal pieces. Place an espresso bean in the center of each piece. Refrigerate until ready to serve.

16 SERVINGS

APPROXIMATE NUTRITIONAL ANALYSIS PER SERVING:

221 calories, 14g total fat, 8g saturated fat, 137mg cholesterol, 23mg sodium, 21g carbohydrates, 3g protein

MOCHA CRÈME

This rich, espresso-flavored buttercream can be used to frost cakes and pastries.

3 large egg yolks
1/2 cup granulated sugar
1/4 cup water
1 cup (2 sticks) unsalted butter, at room temperature
4 tablespoons Espresso Concentrate (page 83)

In a large mixing bowl, lightly beat the egg yolks. In a small saucepan, mix together the sugar and water. Bring to a rolling boil, stirring constantly until the sugar dissolves. Remove from the heat and pour into a small Pyrex measure. Let cool 5 minutes, then pour one-third of the syrup into the bowl with the egg yolks. Using an electric mixer at high speed, beat until incorporated. Stop the mixer and add another one-third of the syrup. Beat again on high, until blended. Stop the mixer and pour in the remaining syrup. Continue beating at high speed until completely cool.

Gradually beat in the butter until well blended. Slowly pour in the espresso concentrate and mix to blend, scraping down the sides with a rubber spatula. The crème can be used immediately or refrigerated for later use. Bring to room temperature before using.

Note: Because this recipe contains raw egg yolks, avoid serving it to anyone to whom the risk of salmonella may cause health-related complications.

APPROXIMATELY 2 CUPS

APPROXIMATE NUTRITIONAL ANALYSIS PER 2 CUPS OF FROSTING:

2193 calories, 199g total fat, 119g saturated fat, 1133mg cholesterol, 52mg sodium, 101g carbohydrates, 10g protein

Tiramisù

Every once in a while we all need a pick-me-up, and that is literally what *tiramisù* is: "pick-me-up" in Italian. This mixture of custard, espresso, and Italian biscuits will definitely lift up the most crestfallen.

- 4 large eggs, lightly beaten
- 1⅓ cups granulated sugar
- 2 tablespoons sweet Marsala wine or sherry
- 1 pound (500 grams) mascarpone cheese (see note)
- 2 tablespoons milk
- 8 Espresso (12 ounces total, page 45), hot
- Approximately 36 savoiardi (Italian ladyfingers; see note)
- 3 tablespoons unsweetened cocoa powder

In the top of a double boiler, whisk together the eggs, 1 cup of the sugar, and the sweet wine until blended. Cook over simmering water, whisking constantly, 3 to 5 minutes, or until the mixture is light and foamy and reaches 160°F on an instant-read thermometer. Remove the custard from the heat immediately and pour into a large mixing bowl. Beat with an electric mixer until thick and cool. In another large bowl, beat the mascarpone and milk with the electric mixer for 1 minute. Fold in the cooled egg mixture. Cover and chill in the refrigerator at least 2 hours or overnight.

Prepare a syrup by mixing the hot espresso with the remaining ⅓ cup sugar. Let cool to room temperature.

To assemble the tiramisù, dip the savoiardi, one at a time, in the espresso syrup and line the bottom of a 13- by 9-inch shallow glass or ceramic baking dish. Fill in all the cracks with pieces of moistened savoiardi, spreading evenly with a spatula. Spoon half of the mascarpone mixture over the savoiardi. Repeat the above steps with the remaining savoiardi and cream, pouring any remaining espresso syrup over the savoiardi before covering with the cream. Cover with plastic wrap and chill at least 6 hours.

Before serving, sprinkle the cocoa powder through a fine sieve or tea strainer over the entire surface of the tiramisù.

Note: Mascarpone cheese and savoiardi are available in most Italian specialty food stores and at some supermarkets.

12 SERVINGS

APPROXIMATE NUTRITIONAL ANALYSIS PER SERVING:

425 calories, 24g total fat, 21g saturated fat, 192mg cholesterol, 72mg sodium, 44g carbohydrates, 8g protein

A cup of coffee—real coffee—home browned, home-ground, home made, that comes to you dark as a hazel-eye, but changes to a golden bronze as you temper it with cream that never cheated, but was real cream from its birth, thick, tenderly yellow, perfectly sweet, neither lumpy nor frothing on the Java: such a cup of coffee is a match for twenty blue devils and will exorcise them all.

—HENRY WARD BEECHER

Pastiera Napoletana

While working on the recipes for this cookbook, I decided that they would all contain espresso in some shape, form, or amount. Well, the following recipe is an exception. Pastiera napoletana is the classic Neapolitan version of Italian cheesecake made with ricotta. Enjoyed by almost everyone, at least at one time or another, in an Italian restaurant or café, it is the perfect accompaniment to a cup of espresso or cappuccino.

This recipe is from my mother, Frances Porretta, one of the best cooks that I know and the one person who has influenced my culinary skills and interest the most. The recipe has been in our family for as long as I can remember. In fact, it has special significance for me, since it was the first thing that I ever tried my hand at as a child helping my mother in the kitchen. Every Saturday before Easter it was my job to press the crust into the pans while my mother prepared the filling.

Over the years my mother has become known for her wonderful pastiera napoletana as well as her pizza rustica—and rightfully so.

Crust

2 cups unbleached all-purpose flour
2/3 cup granulated sugar
1/4 teaspoon salt
3/4 cup (1 1/2 sticks) unsalted butter, chilled and cut into small pieces
1 large egg, lightly beaten
1 tablespoon milk

Filling

1/2 cup hulled wheat kernels or 1 can (15 ounces) wheat kernels (see note)
1 1/2 pounds whole-milk ricotta
1/4 cup unbleached all-purpose flour
1 cup granulated sugar
Pinch of salt
4 large eggs
2 tablespoons orange flower water (see note)
1 tablespoon vanilla extract

Prepare the crust: Sift together the flour, sugar, and salt into a large mixing bowl. Rub in the cold butter with your fingertips until the mixture is dry and crumbly. Mix together

the egg and milk and add to the flour and butter mixture. Mix with your hands just until the dough starts to come together in a ball. Wrap in plastic wrap and refrigerate at least 1 hour, or until chilled.

Prepare the filling: If using dry wheat kernels, begin to prepare them 2 days before you plan to bake the pastiera. Soak the wheat overnight. Drain and rinse the next day and place in a medium-size saucepan. Cover with water and bring to a boil. Lower the heat to a simmer and cook, covered, until the kernels are tender, approximately 1 to 1½ hours. Check periodically and add additional water as needed. Remove from the heat and cool to room temperature.

In a large mixing bowl, beat the ricotta until creamy, using an electric hand mixer. Gradually add the flour, sugar, and salt. Beat in the eggs, one at a time. Add the orange flower water and vanilla. Beat until well blended and creamy. Fold in the cooked wheat kernels. Set aside.

Preheat the oven to 350°F. Lightly butter a 9-by 2-inch round cake pan.

Assemble the pastiera: Remove the chilled crust from the refrigerator. Tear off walnut-size pieces of crust and flatten between your fingertips. Starting in the center of the pan, press the flattened piece of crust into the bottom of the pan. Repeat the process with the remaining dough, covering the bottom and sides, making sure that the pieces overlap. Flatten the dough with your fingertips so that it is approximately ⅛ inch thick all around. Press the dough up the sides of the pan so there is a slight overhang. Slice off excess dough with a sharp knife so that the top edge is clean.

Pour in the prepared filling and bake approximately 45 to 55 minutes, or until the filling is set and the pastry is golden. Cool on a wire rack.

Usually we serve the pastiera in the pan in which it was baked to avoid the risk of it cracking. Sprinkle with confectioners' sugar before serving, if desired.

Note: Wheat kernels and orange flower water are available in most Italian specialty stores and at some health food stores.

10 SERVINGS

APPROXIMATE NUTRITIONAL ANALYSIS PER SERVING:

538 calories, 15g total fat, 15g saturated fat, 178mg cholesterol, 177mg sodium, 63g carbohydrates, 15g protein

Espresso Rum Charlotte

Many famous culinary creations were originally made for royalty. The original charlotte russe, a wonderful dessert made of ladyfingers and pastry cream, was created for Czar Alexander of Russia. This Italian version is equally delicious. The crisp savoiardi biscuits are dipped in the diluted rum and are then covered with a layer of espresso custard and whipped cream. A very simple, yet elegant dessert.

- 1/4 cup (1/2 stick) unsalted butter, melted
- 1/4 cup light brown sugar, packed
- 1 large egg
- 1 Espresso (1 1/2 ounces, page 45) at room temperature
- 1 package (7 ounces) savoiardi (Italian ladyfingers; page 126)
- 1/4 cup dark rum
- 1/2 cup water
- 1 cup heavy cream, sweetened with 1 tablespoon granulated sugar and whipped to soft peaks
- 3 tablespoons sliced almonds, toasted

In the top of a double boiler, whisk together the melted butter, brown sugar, egg, and espresso until well blended. Cook 2 to 3 minutes over simmering water, whisking constantly, until the mixture just begins to thicken. Remove from the heat and pour into a small mixing bowl. Cover with a piece of plastic wrap, pushing the plastic into the custard so that a skin does not form. Let cool to room temperature.

In a shallow bowl mix together the rum and water. Dip the savoiardi quickly in the diluted rum and line the bottom of a 10- by 8-inch baking dish. Spoon the custard over the savoiardi, spreading evenly with a spatula. Layer with the remaining savoiardi dipped in the rum mixture. Pour any remaining diluted rum over the savoiardi before covering with the whipped cream. Cover evenly with the cream and sprinkle with the almonds. Cover with plastic wrap and chill at least 3 hours before serving.

6 SERVINGS

APPROXIMATE NUTRITIONAL ANALYSIS PER SERVING:

339 calories, 20g total fat, 11g saturated fat, 204mg cholesterol, 148mg sodium, 29g carbohydrates, 6g protein

It's easier to change one's religion than to change one's coffee. Moreover, the world is divided into two: those who patronize cafés and those who never set foot in them. From this derive two different frames of mind, quite separate and distinct; and one of which—that of those who frequently go to cafés—seems to me quite superior to the other one.

—GEORGES COURTELINE

Cappuccino Mousse

This very elegant dessert is quick and easy to make. Since it has to chill so that the gelatin thickens, be sure to prepare it early in the day.

- 1½ teaspoons unflavored gelatin
- 4 Espresso (6 ounces total, page 45), at room temperature
- 2 large egg yolks, lightly beaten
- 8 ounces white chocolate, chopped or morsels
- 2 cups heavy cream
- ¼ cup granulated sugar

In a small saucepan, sprinkle the gelatin over the espresso. Set aside.

In the top of a double boiler over simmering water, melt the chocolate. Pour into a large mixing bowl. Place the espresso mixture over low heat and stir until the gelatin is completely dissolved. Add the egg yolks, whisking constantly, 3 to 5 minutes, or until the mixture is light and reaches 160°F on an instant-read thermometer. Do not let boil or the eggs will curdle. Remove from the heat and fold into the melted chocolate. Let cool to room temperature.

Whip the heavy cream until thickened. Gradually add the sugar and continue whipping to soft peaks. Gently fold the espresso mixture into the whipped cream. Spoon into a large serving bowl or individual dessert dishes. Cover and chill at least 2 hours.

Note: The 160°F temperature is necessary for avoiding the risk of salmonella from the eggs.

8 SERVINGS

APPROXIMATE NUTRITIONAL ANALYSIS PER SERVING:

416 calories, 32g total fat, 19g saturated fat, 141mg cholesterol, 49mg sodium, 31g carbohydrates, 4g protein

Espresso Crème Brûlée

Crème brûlée is a classic French dessert of egg custard sprinkled with sugar that is quickly caramelized to form a thin brittle topping. The contrast of the smooth custard and the crunchy topping is a real taste treat. The addition of coffee adds to the complexity of the flavors.

- 3 cups light cream
- 1/3 cup espresso beans, coarsely crushed
- 6 tablespoons granulated sugar
- 3 large eggs plus 3 large egg yolks
- 6 tablespoons light brown sugar, packed, for sprinkling

Preheat the oven to 300°F and place the baking rack in the lowest shelf position. Place six 6-ounce ramekins or broiler-proof custard cups in a shallow baking pan.

In a medium-size saucepan, bring the cream and coffee beans to a boil. Remove from the heat, cover, and let cool 15 minutes.

In a medium-size bowl, beat together the eggs, egg yolks, and granulated sugar. Set aside. Pour the cream through a fine-mesh strainer into a clean medium-size saucepan and bring to a boil. Discard the coffee beans. Lower the heat under the cream and gradually whisk in the egg mixture. Cook over medium heat for 3 minutes, stirring constantly so that the custard does not burn.

Pour the mixture into the ramekins or custard cups. Place the pan in the oven and pour boiling water in the pan so that the water is halfway up the sides of the cups. Bake until the custard is set, approximately 40 minutes. Remove the custards from the pan and let cool to room temperature, about 1 hour.

Preheat the broiler.

Sprinkle the tops of the custards with 1 tablespoon each of brown sugar. Gently pat the sugar down. Place under the broiler for 2 to 3 minutes, or just until the sugar begins to melt and bubble. Let cool and refrigerate at least 30 minutes before serving.

6 SERVINGS

APPROXIMATE NUTRITIONAL ANALYSIS PER SERVING:

498 calories, 42g total fat, 25g saturated fat, 345mg cholesterol, 80mg sodium, 25g carbohydrates, 7g protein

Espresso Flan

While there are many wonderful desserts and confections to choose from in Spain, flan is probably the best known. Espresso flan is a variation of this Spanish dessert. Rather than line the pan with caramelized sugar, the pan is coated with Espresso Syrup. To ensure that the syrup does not mix with the custard mixture, the syrup must be frozen in the pan for at least 2 hours beforehand, so plan accordingly.

6 tablespoons Espresso Syrup (page 84)
2 cups milk
6 large eggs
3/4 cup granulated sugar

Before making the flan, pour the syrup into the bottom of a perfectly flat 9-inch round cake pan. Swirl to cover the bottom. Place in the freezer for 2 hours, or until frozen.

Preheat the oven to 350°F.

Heat the milk in a medium-size saucepan until it begins to boil. Remove from the heat. In a large mixing bowl, whisk together the eggs and sugar. Gradually pour in the hot milk and whisk together until well blended. Pour the custard into the prepared pan and set in a larger cake pan. Place in the oven and fill the larger pan with boiling water to halfway up the sides of the cake pan. Bake approximately 1 hour, 15 minutes, or until the custard is set.

Remove the flan from the water bath and let cool to room temperature. Refrigerate, in the pan, until cold, about 2 hours. To serve, run a sharp knife around the edge of the flan and invert onto a serving dish. Cut into wedges and drizzle with syrup from the flan.

8 SERVINGS

APPROXIMATE NUTRITIONAL ANALYSIS PER SERVING:

181 calories, 4g total fat, 2g saturated fat, 161mg cholesterol, 79mg sodium, 29g carbohydrates, 7g protein

Cappuccino Bread Pudding

This variation on traditional bread pudding is perfect to serve at breakfast or brunch or for dessert after a light dinner. Serve alone or perhaps with a small pitcher of Crème Anglaise Café (opposite page) to pour on the side.

- 4 cups ½-inch cubes good-quality day-old white or egg bread with the crusts removed
- 6 large eggs plus 4 large egg yolks
- ½ cup granulated sugar
- ¼ cup Espresso Syrup (page 84)
- 3 cups half-and-half

Preheat the oven to 325°F. Butter a 10-cup baking dish.

Evenly spread the bread cubes in the prepared dish. In a large mixing bowl, whisk together the eggs, egg yolks, sugar, syrup, and half-and-half. Pour the custard mixture over the bread, making sure all the bread cubes are covered. Let stand 30 minutes.

Place baking dish in a shallow baking pan. Place in the oven and fill the pan with enough boiling water to come halfway up the side of the baking dish. Bake approximately 55 minutes, or until the center is set.

10 SERVINGS

APPROXIMATE NUTRITIONAL ANALYSIS PER SERVING:

271 calories, 14g total fat, 7g saturated fat, 240mg cholesterol, 168mg sodium, 27g carbohydrates, 9g protein

Crème Anglaise Café

Crème anglaise is a classic French custard sauce that can be served either hot or cold over cake, fruit, or other desserts. Serve with plain pound cake or with Cappuccino Bread Pudding (opposite page).

- 1 cup milk
- 3 tablespoons espresso beans, coarsely crushed
- 4 large egg yolks
- 3 tablespoons granulated sugar
- 1 tablespoon Espresso Syrup (page 84)

In a medium-size saucepan, bring the milk and espresso beans to a boil. Remove from the heat, cover, and let sit 15 minutes. Pour into a small Pyrex measure through a fine-mesh strainer. Discard the coffee beans.

In the top of a double boiler, whisk together the egg yolks and sugar until well blended. Pour the warm coffee-flavored milk into the egg yolk mixture. Heat the mixture over simmering water, sitting constantly. Remove from the heat when the crème just begins to coat the back of the spoon. Pour into a small bowl, cover and chill in the refrigerator. Whisk in the syrup just before serving.

Serve within 3 days.

APPROXIMATELY 1½ CUPS

APPROXIMATE NUTRITIONAL ANALYSIS PER ¼-CUP SERVING:

87 calories, 4g total fat, 1g saturated fat, 143mg cholesterol, 25mg sodium, 10g carbohydrates, 3g protein

Mocha Mint Chocolate-Chip Cookies

Coffee, chocolate, and mint have an affinity for each other. When combined together in a cookie they create a sublime taste treat.

- 1 cup (2 sticks) unsalted butter, at room temperature
- 1 1/2 cups granulated sugar
- 2 large eggs
- 1 teaspoon mint extract
- 1/4 cup Espresso Concentrate (page 83)
- 2 cups unbleached all-purpose flour
- 2/3 cup unsweetened cocoa powder
- 1 teaspoon baking soda
- 12 ounces mini chocolate chips

Preheat the oven to 350°F. Butter two baking sheets.

Cream the butter and sugar together until the mixture is light, using an electric mixer. Add the eggs, mint extract, and espresso concentrate. Beat well. Add the flour, cocoa powder, and baking soda. Mix well. Fold in the chocolate chips.

Drop the dough by rounded teaspoonfuls, 2 inches apart, on the prepared baking sheets. Press down lightly. Bake 10 to 12 minutes, or until lightly browned.

APPROXIMATELY 72 COOKIES

APPROXIMATE NUTRITIONAL ANALYSIS PER COOKIE:

78 calories, 4g total fat, 3g saturated fat, 13mg cholesterol, 14mg sodium, 10g carbohydrates, 1g protein

If this is coffee, please bring me some tea;
if this is tea, please bring me some coffee.

—ABRAHAM LINCOLN

Coffee Meringues

Meringues, one of the world's oldest confections, make their appearance in almost every cuisine in the Western world. When preparing custards and creams calling for egg yolks only, why not save the whites and whip up a batch of these coffee-flavored meringues?

1 cup granulated sugar
1/4 cup water
3 large egg whites
2 tablespoons Espresso Concentrate (page 83)
Confectioners' sugar for sprinkling

Set racks in the upper and lower thirds of the oven. Preheat the oven to 300°F. Line two baking sheets with baking parchment.

In a medium-size saucepan, mix together the sugar and water. Bring to a boil. Lower to a simmer and continue cooking, without stirring, for 10 minutes or until thick. Remove from the heat and let cool 10 minutes.

In a large mixing bowl, beat the egg whites with an electric mixer while very slowly pouring in the hot sugar syrup. Make sure not to pour the hot syrup on the metal beaters, since the syrup will harden on contact. Beat until the egg whites form very stiff, shiny peaks. Gently fold in the espresso concentrate.

Drop the meringues by rounded teaspoonfuls, 2 inches apart, on the prepared cookie sheets. Bake 35 to 40 minutes, or until golden brown. Let cool completely, on the baking sheets, on a wire rack, before removing.

APPROXIMATELY 32 COOKIES

APPROXIMATE NUTRITIONAL ANALYSIS PER COOKIE:

26 calories, 0g total fat, 0g saturated fat, 0mg cholesterol, 5mg sodium, 6g carbohydrates, 0g protein

Mocha Biscotti with Nuts

Over the past few years Italian biscotti have been appearing everywhere—and no wonder. These twice-baked, mocha-flavored nut cookies will satisfy any sweet tooth.

- 2¼ cups unbleached all-purpose flour
- ½ cup unsweetened cocoa powder
- 1 teaspoon baking powder
- ¼ teaspoon baking soda
- ¼ teaspoon salt
- ½ cup whole hazelnuts, toasted, with any loose skin rubbed off
- ½ cup slivered almonds
- 1 cup granulated sugar
- ¼ cup (½ stick) unsalted butter, at room temperature
- 3 large eggs, lightly beaten
- ¼ cup Espresso Concentrate (page 83)

Preheat the oven to 375°F.

In a large bowl, sift together the flour, cocoa powder, baking powder, baking soda, and salt. Add the hazelnuts and almonds. Set aside.

In a large mixing bowl, mix together the butter and sugar until small crumbs form, using an electric mixer set on medium. Gradually add the beaten eggs and the espresso concentrate. Set the mixer on low and gradually add the flour mixture. Stop mixing once a smooth, soft dough forms.

Using the side of a wooden spoon, divide the dough into two equal parts. Spoon each part of dough onto one side of a large baking sheet covered with baking parchment or lightly buttered. Using your hands, shape each part into a thin, smooth log about 2 inches in diameter by 12 inches long.

Bake approximately 20 minutes, or until lightly browned underneath. Remove the baking sheet from the oven. Carefully remove the baked logs from the pan and place on a cutting board. Using a very sharp utility or chef's knife, cut each hot log crosswise on the diagonal into ½-inch-wide slices. Lay as many slices as can fit on their sides on the cookie sheet and bake another 8 to 10 minutes, or until the biscotti are dry and crisp. Repeat with the remaining biscotti. Remove from the baking sheet and let cool on a wire rack before storing in airtight containers.

APPROXIMATELY 4 DOZEN BISCOTTI

APPROXIMATE NUTRITIONAL ANALYSIS PER COOKIE:

54 calories, 3g total fat, 1g saturated fat, 16mg cholesterol, 30mg sodium, 6g carbohydrates, 2g protein

POACHED WINTER FRUIT

Traditionally, poached fruit was served during the long months of winter, when fresh fruits were unavailable. Frugal housewives would air-dry fruit from their orchards to be enjoyed later in the year in compotes and pastries.

The addition of anise seed and lemon peel to the following recipe for poached fruit adds a delicious Mediterranean touch to this simple, yet elegant dessert.

- 2 cups water
- 1/2 cup granulated sugar
- 1/2 teaspoon anise seed
- Zest of 1 lemon cut in a continuous strip
- 1/2 cup dried Calimyrna or Smyrna figs, halved
- 1/2 cup dried pitted prunes
- 1/2 cup dried apricots
- 1/2 cup dried peaches, quartered
- 1/2 cup dried pears, quartered
- 1/2 cup golden raisins
- 2 tablespoons Espresso Syrup (page 84)

Combine the water, sugar, anise seed, and lemon zest in a large saucepan and bring to a boil. Lower the heat and simmer 10 minutes, uncovered. Remove from the heat and add the dried fruit. Stir to mix. Cover and let sit several hours or overnight in the refrigerator. Bring to room temperature, stir in the syrup, and serve.

8 SERVINGS

APPROXIMATE NUTRITIONAL ANALYSIS PER SERVING:

156 calories, 0g total fat, 0g saturated fat, 0mg cholesterol, 5mg sodium, 40g carbohydrates, 1g protein

Coffee is a fleeting moment and a fragrance.

—CLAUDIA RODEN

Espresso Sweets and Candies

Having a very pronounced sweet tooth, I have always enjoyed making and eating homemade candy, especially chocolates and candies that are chewy or made with nuts.

Coffee is used by confectioners to intensify the flavor of chocolate without overpowering it. It is wonderful how the rich flavors of both play off the other, adding depth and complexity. This is especially evident with Chocolate-Covered Espresso Beans. On the other hand, milk and cream always add smoothness and round out the rich flavor of espresso when combined in hot drink combinations, which led me to develop the Coffee and Milk Caramels. Highly addictive and chewy, each bite tastes like a sip of cappuccino.

Chocolate-Covered Espresso Beans

Chocolate-covered espresso beans are quite simply addictive. The chocolate fudge–like covering lends a soft foil to the crunchy espresso bean hiding within.

- 1/4 cup espresso beans, sorted (whole beans only)
- 6 ounces semisweet chocolate, chopped or morsels
- 3 tablespoons light corn syrup

Preheat the oven to 375°F.

Toast the espresso beans on a baking sheet for 15 minutes.

Meanwhile, melt the chocolate in the top of a double boiler over simmering water. Remove from the heat and stir in the corn syrup. The mixture will appear grainy. Continue stirring until smooth and the mixture begins to form a ball. Let cool to room temperature. Cover and chill in the refrigerator 30 minutes.

Tear off small pieces of chocolate the size of a large pea and wrap each around a toasted espresso bean. Roll between the palms of your hands until smooth and slightly oval. Place on a pan covered with wax paper. Refrigerate until firm. Store the chocolate-covered espresso beans in a shallow, airtight container in the refrigerator up to 2 weeks.

APPROXIMATELY 150 CHOCOLATE-COVERED ESPRESSO BEANS

APPROXIMATE NUTRITIONAL ANALYSIS PER SERVING OF 5 BEANS:

33 calories, 2g total fat, 1g saturated fat, 0mg cholesterol, 3mg sodium, 5g carbohydrates, 0g protein

Mocha Truffles

Truffles have become very popular in this country over the past few years. The following recipe is a personal favorite, one that I make every holiday season without fail. For best results, use only good-quality milk chocolate.

12 ounces milk chocolate, chopped or morsels
1/4 cup (1/2 stick) unsalted butter
1/2 cup heavy cream
1/4 cup Espresso Syrup (page 84)
Unsweetened cocoa powder for coating

Put the chocolate and butter in the top of a double boiler over simmering water. Cover until melted. Beat with a whisk to blend. Add the cream and whisk until well blended. Pour in the syrup and whisk together. Remove from the heat and pour the truffle mixture into a nonreactive bowl. Let cool to room temperature. Chill, covered, in the refrigerator until firm.

Using a melon baller or teaspoon, scoop out a small amount of the truffle mixture and quickly roll it between the palms of your hands until round. Roll in the cocoa powder and chill in the refrigerator until firm again. Truffles can be stored for up to 1 week in the refrigerator in an airtight container.

Note: Traditionally, truffles are made with semisweet or bittersweet chocolate. I find that milk chocolate works best in this recipe, since the combination of dark chocolate and espresso is too intense.

APPROXIMATELY 48 TRUFFLES

APPROXIMATE NUTRITIONAL ANALYSIS PER TRUFFLE:

52 calories, 4g total fat, 3g saturated fat, 6mg cholesterol, 12mg sodium, 5g carbohydrates, 1g protein

Coffee and Milk Caramels

These wonderfully chewy caramels are rich in coffee and cream. If you do not yet have a candy thermometer, now is the time to purchase one, since the temperature of the caramel mixture is the key to good results.

1 cup granulated sugar
2/3 cup light corn syrup
5 Espresso (7 1/2 ounces total, page 45)
1/2 cup heavy cream

Lightly oil an 8-inch square baking pan. In a medium-size saucepan, bring the sugar, corn syrup, and espresso to a boil over high heat. Stir down with a wooden spoon as the mixture begins to rise up. After the foaming subsides, let cook, covered, 5 minutes, or until a candy thermometer registers 234°F (soft ball stage). Carefully pour in the cream while stirring and stir continuously for approximately 3 to 5 minutes, or until the mixture appears thick and registers 244°F (firm ball stage) on a candy thermometer. Remove from the heat immediately and pour the caramel mixture into the prepared pan. Let cool to room temperature.

When the caramel mixture has set, cut into 1-inch squares with a sharp kitchen knife. Store in single layers in airtight containers lined with greased wax paper.

APPROXIMATELY 64 CARAMELS

APPROXIMATE NUTRITIONAL ANALYSIS PER CARAMEL:

28 calories, 1g total fat, 1g saturated fat, 3mg cholesterol, 5mg sodium, 6g carbohydrates, 0g protein

Coffee is a pleasure. . . . If it isn't excellent, where's the pleasure?

—LUIGI LAVAZZA

Espresso Almond Brittle

Almond brittle of any kind is a personal favorite.

1 cup (2 sticks) unsalted butter
3/4 cup coarsely chopped blanched almonds
1 1/4 cups granulated sugar
1 cup (6 ounces) milk chocolate chips
2 tablespoons Espresso Concentrate (page 83)

Lightly oil a 13- by 9-inch baking pan. Melt the butter in a medium-size saucepan over medium heat. Add the almonds and sugar and raise the heat to high, stirring continuously with a wooden spoon. As the mixture heats up and cooks, the sugar will go through various changes. At first it will look very granular. It will then melt and become granular again, and the butter may appear to separate from the mixture. Continue cooking, stirring continuously, and the sugar will once again melt. The mixture is ready when it looks like melted peanut butter. Remove from the heat at once or the almonds will burn. Pour into the prepared pan, spreading as evenly as possible with a spatula. Set aside.

In the top of a double boiler over simmering water, melt the chocolate. Blend in the espresso concentrate. Pour over the hardening candy and spread evenly. Let cool to room temperature.

Remove the candy by inverting the pan. Break the candy into small pieces.

APPROXIMATELY 48 PIECES

APPROXIMATE NUTRITIONAL ANALYSIS PER PIECE:

83 calories, 6g total fat, 3g saturated fat, 11mg cholesterol, 4mg sodium, 8g carbohydrates, 1g protein

The best maxim I know in life, is to drink your coffee when you can, and when you cannot, to be easy without it.

—Jonathan Swift

TROUBLESHOOTING GUIDE TO PERFECT ESPRESSO AND FROTHED MILK

For best results, be sure to read and refer to the Introduction, especially pages 30 to 39, and to all printed and visual materials provided by the manufacturer of your espresso machine.

PROBLEM

Coffee drips over the sides of the filter holder.

REASON

1. Too much coffee was used.
2. Filter holder not properly positioned or locked in place.
3. Diffuser or filter holder blocked.
4. Clogged filter holder spouts.
5. Leaky gasket.

SOLUTION

1. Do not overfill the filter with too much coffee, which will inhibit the filter holder from being properly locked into place.
2. Holding the filter holder straight, push up and then turn in the direction indicated by the manufacturer required to lock in place.

3. Always clean the diffuser of any stuck-on grounds after making espresso. Wipe with a clean, damp kitchen cloth or sponge. The filter should always be rinsed under cold water to wash away any grounds that can clog the filter.
4. Check to make certain the filter holder spouts are not clogged. Always rinse under water after each use. Clean out periodically with a pipe cleaner, or soak in water.
5. Consult with the manufacturer regarding replacing the rubber gasket located around the diffuser.

PROBLEM

Coffee comes out too fast or crema is pale.

REASON

1. Coffee is ground too coarse.
2. Espresso roast/blend not used.
3. Insufficient amount of coffee.
4. Too-light tamping.

SOLUTION

1. Use only finely ground coffee. Coffee should be as fine as table salt.
2. Use only coffee roasted and blended for espresso machines. Try changing blends or brand until the desired results are achieved.
3. Always use the right size filter for the desired amount of coffee. Always fill the filter with the correct amount of coffee.
4. Tamp harder so that coffee is more compressed.

PROBLEM

Coffee trickles too slowly or not at all *or* crema is too dark.

REASON

1. Coffee is ground too fine.
2. Too much coffee.
3. Too-heavy tamping.

SOLUTION

1. Use a slightly coarser grind of coffee. Coffee should be as coarse as table salt.
2. Always use the right size filter for the desired amount of coffee. Use less coffee; always fill the filter with the correct amount of coffee.
3. Tamp more lightly so that the coffee is not so compressed.

PROBLEM

There are coffee grounds in the cup.

REASON

1. Coffee ground too fine.
2. Coffee on filter holder.

SOLUTION

1. Use a slightly coarser grind of coffee. Coffee should be as coarse as table salt.
2. After placing the coffee in the filter, wipe any spilled grounds off the filter holder.

PROBLEM

Coffee grounds are wet and muddy in the filter after brewing coffee.

REASON

1. Diffuser blocked.
2. Filter holder spouts are partially blocked.

SOLUTION

1. Always clean the diffuser of any stuck-on grounds after making espresso. Wipe with a clean, damp kitchen cloth or sponge.
2. Check to make certain that the filter holder spouts are not clogged. Always rinse under water after each use. Clean out periodically with a pipe cleaner, or soak in water.

PROBLEM

Very little steam to froth or steam milk.

REASON

1. Espresso machine is not hot enough to produce steam.
2. If using a steam espresso machine, too much time has passed between brewing espresso and frothing or steaming milk.
3. Holes in frothing wand are clogged.

SOLUTION

1. Always allow the espresso machine to heat up sufficiently before attempting to froth or steam milk.
2. Always froth or steam milk immediately after brewing espresso.
3. The frothing wand must always be kept clean. Wipe with a clean, damp kitchen cloth after frothing or steaming to remove any milk residue. Open clogged holes with a straight pin.

PROBLEM

Milk does not produce enough froth.

REASON

Milk is too hot.

SOLUTION

Follow frothing instructions given on page 38. Do not overheat milk to point of scalding, which reduces froth. Do not try to re-froth milk that has been previously frothed.

CREDITS

I want to thank all of the espresso machine manufacturers listed who kindly provided me with espresso machines to use in developing this book and the recipes. For your convenience, I have provided the manufacturers' customer service phone numbers.

Braun, Inc.
800-272-8611

Briel America, Inc.
201-716-0999

DeLonghi America, Inc.
800-322-3848

Gaggia/Lello Appliances Corp.
800-642-4414

Krups North America, Inc.
800-526-5377

La Pavoni/European Gift & Houseware
800-927-0277

Melitta North America
800-451-1694

Mr. Coffee, Inc.
800-MR. COFFEE

Rancilio/Saeco USA, Inc.
800-437-0874

Rowenta, Inc.
617-396-0600, ex. 400

Saeco USA, Inc.
800-437-0874

Salton/MAXIM Housewares, Inc.
800-233-9054

In addition to providing me with their espresso machines, I also wish to acknowledge Krups for the La Glacière ice cream maker that I used in developing the ice cream and frozen dessert recipes and for the cross-section illustrations that were adapted for use on pages 28, 29, and 30.

Special thanks to Gloria Smith of the Zanger Company (800-229-4687) for providing the beautiful Bunzlauer stoneware holding the Caffè Macchiato (facing page 65) and to Angelo Forzano of European Gift & Houseware (800-927-0277) who, besides offering expert advice on espresso, provided the authentic Italian espresso and cappuccino cups shown in the photo of the espresso machines on the back cover.

Special credit is given to Lavazza Premium Coffees (800-466-3287) who, in addition to giving invaluable information on coffee and espresso, kept me well stocked with their wonderful whole-bean and ground espresso coffees while working on this book.

INDEX

Page numbers in **boldface** refer to recipes.